HEALED FOR HOLINESS

Healed for Holiness

*The Role of Inner Healing
in the Christian Life*

Martin and Sally Lynch

SERVANT BOOKS
Ann Arbor, Michigan

Cover design by Steve Eames

Published by Servant Books
P.O. Box 8617
Ann Arbor, Michigan 48107

Printed in the United States of America
ISBN 0-89283-275-4
88 89 90 91 92 10 9 8 7 6 5 4 3 2 1

For love of the King

Contents

Foreword
by
Fr. Michael Scanlan, T.O.R.

MARTIN AND SALLY LYNCH take on the challenge of communicating God's great gift of inner healing in *Healed for Holiness*. I know how much of a challenge it is because I wrote a book titled *Inner Healing* back in 1974.

At that time, the challenge was to distinguish inner healing from counseling, sensitivity sessions, and deliverance by showing that it is meant to be an integral part of the healing ministry. Physical healing was just being introduced to Catholics as something which could be experienced "at home" in your local parish or prayer group. It was not confined to Lourdes or the lives of saints and mystics. Inner healing had to be presented as a logical extension of physical healing, flowing from the same source and based on the same spiritual principles.

For Martin and Sally, the challenge is different. Inner healing is now widely accepted as a fact. Indeed, there seems to be more acceptance of inner healing than physical healing. The challenge today is to communicate the good news that inner healing is for *you*. In other words, each person can receive this gift in his or her own life. Also, inner healing must be understood within the broader context of spiritual warfare and the pursuit of holiness.

In *Healed for Holiness*, the Lynches meet the challenge for today and are well qualified to do so. They have combined professional therapy and a powerful inner healing ministry to care for God's people over the past fifteen years. They have taught widely and directed a large association of Christian therapists. Martin and Sally have the background and experience to speak with authority.

The Lynches write about God's healing in their own lives and draw upon case studies from their ministry to illustrate important principles for inner healing. They teach with authority in *Healed for Holiness,* yet the instruction is so skillfully interwoven with stories that at times it is barely noticed. The central message of their book is that the role of inner healing is to help us respond to God's call, which is a call to holiness.

Martin and Sally have given us a simple and very readable presentation of their experiences and insights on inner healing. They treat inner healing as a gift of God which they have joyfully received and don't need to justify. They do not argue positions or cite authorities. They simply present the good news of God's blessings in healing, even in suffering, and in growing in holiness. *Healed for Holiness* meets the challenge of our day to communicate convincingly how much God desires a whole and *holy* people.

Introduction

IF ONE THING IS CLEAR ABOUT the area of healing, even from a quick reading of Scripture, it is the simple truth that God heals people who call upon him. We see this especially in the New Testament which gives us numerous examples of the healing of sick bodies, minds, and spirits. Most of these are people healed by Jesus during his three years of public ministry.

But the gift of healing also characterizes the lives of Jesus' followers after his ascension and the descent of the Holy Spirit at Pentecost. The apostle Peter heals a crippled beggar at the temple gate called Beautiful and boldly proclaims the gospel, for example (Acts 3). Over twenty years after Pentecost, Paul writes to the early Christians at Corinth about the use of the spiritual gifts. In his letter, he lists healing and the working of miracles among the spiritual gifts (1 Cor 12).

We can see from Scripture that God's power to heal and his desire to heal transformed the lives of many men and women. The centuries of Christian history which have followed the New Testament era reveal the same striking truth. Although it sometimes goes unnoticed, healing has not been infrequent in Christian history. Many of the great revivals associated with holy men and women of God, religious orders, revival preachers, and renewal movements have been marked by miraculous healings.

For instance, Anthony of Padua, a Franciscan friar in

the thirteenth century, was a power-filled preacher whose compelling words were routinely accompanied by signs and wonders. Within one year of his death on June 13, 1231, no less than forty-six miracles attributed to his ministry had passed the rigorous scrutiny of church officials investigating his popular acclaim. The wonder-worker of Padua was part of a larger revival spearheaded by Francis of Assisi, a revival that turned the known world upside down in the thirteenth century through the power of the Holy Spirit.

In the twentieth century, we have witnessed a great outpouring of God's healing power through the Pentecostal movement and the charismatic renewal. There is a renewed interest in healing as one of the spiritual gifts of the Holy Spirit. We see Christians of all backgrounds anointed for the work of healing among God's people.

Unfortunately, some of the current approaches to healing are contaminated by "New Age" or holistic spirituality. This false religion, which is part of the human potential movement, focuses on the untapped resources within the self and holds out the deceptive promise of wholeness. It draws on occult sources of power, counterfeiting the true satisfaction of a spiritual hunger that only God can fill.

As Christians in need of healing ourselves and as dedicated therapists trained in psychology and psychiatry, we've experienced firsthand God's saving power. We know that only he can fill that gnawing spiritual hunger inside each one of us, not "New Age" spirituality or other false religions.

God's plan for healing does include freedom from emotional and psychological scars. He wants his people whole. Healing is an extraordinary expression of God the Father's divine mercy and love. But we need the perspective of Scripture and Christian tradition to claim God's healing and to understand it. That's the aim of our book. We want to demonstrate how the mercy of God expressed through inner healing is a grace for holiness. We want to bring God's mind and his perspective to our study and experience of healing.

In the Gospel of Luke, we read an account that gives us an inkling of God's eternal perspective on healing: the well-known story of Jesus and the ten lepers. It tells us much about the connection between human disorders, divine healing, wholeness, and holiness.

On his journey to Jerusalem he passed along the borders of Samaria and Galilee. As he was entering a village, ten lepers met him. Keeping their distance, they raised their voices and said, "Jesus, Master, have pity on us!" When he saw them, he responded, "Go and show yourselves to the priests." On their way there they were cured. One of them, realizing that he had been cured, came back praising God in a loud voice. He threw himself on his face at the feet of Jesus and spoke his praises. This man was a Samaritan.

Jesus took the occasion to say, "Were not all ten made whole? Where are the other nine? Was there no one to return and give thanks to God except this foreigner?" He said to the man, "Stand up and go your way; your faith has been your salvation." (Lk 17:11-19)

The case of the ten lepers is very interesting for two reasons. First, anyone who has worked with lepers can tell you that the emotional scars of this disease cause as much distress to the victim as the physical scars and the pain. A leper is so feared and shunned that today the colloquial expression "What am I, a leper?" carries with it the message of "Why are you avoiding and rejecting me?"

Someone healed of leprosy needs to be healed not only of the disease but of deep internal problems caused by a tangle of interpersonal evil like abandonment and rejection by others, even mockery and abuse. On a personal level, the leper usually has a poor self-concept characterized by anger, self-hatred, and despair.

Jesus understands this need for deep inner healing and makes the ten lepers "whole." Their healing is much more than skin deep. In contemporary thinking, the ten experience both physical and inner healing.

Luke the Evangelist makes another important point in the account. He tells us that only the Samaritan returns to thank Jesus and to praise God for his healing. This man who is both a leper and a hated foreigner overcomes a double separation. He is now ready to re-enter earthly society and is also ready for the kingdom of God. His faith in the Jewish Messiah has won him salvation.

The Samaritan's reaction to his healing shows that his mind and heart have been cleansed so he can recognize the true identity of Jesus as healer and Lord. That recognition elicits a free, fitting response: he throws himself at the feet of Jesus, the holy one. He has grasped the important truth that healing is a grace for holiness and conversion.

Through this miraculous event, Luke emphasizes to us the importance of a personal relationship with Jesus. The purpose of healing is not just to make us feel better or to live longer. Healing's purpose is to lead us into a lifelong relationship with the holy one who has the power to change our lives. We learn that healing is meant to call forth not only gratitude but holy awe in the presence of the divine healer. God clearly intends healing as a springboard to reformation and the lifelong pursuit of holiness.

This holy God, who healed the ten lepers and has healed countless others throughout the ages, heals today! In fact, interest in divine healing—including announcements of new healing ministries and miraculous cures—seems quite high in our day.

Yet too much of the time personalities, ministries, and the physical manifestations of healing seem to take center stage. True wholeness and holiness are not emphasized or are even forgotten.

We're grateful God has led us, as a psychologist and a psychiatric nurse, to wholeness and holiness through his healing touch. During the past fifteen years, he has healed both of us of serious illnesses: illnesses that sowed the seeds of physical death and deep emotional trauma.

God's healing work brought restoration to our marriage, our family, and ourselves. He led us to dedicate our careers as health-care professionals to the important work of Christian therapy and inner healing. We feel compelled now more than ever to share this urgent call to conversion and holiness, especially with those who can lead the way in rebuilding the helping and healing professions from the ground floor up.

We'd like to start by sharing our own story of healing. It opens on a blustery autumn day in 1972 when death paid us a surprise visit.

What was our response? Were we ready for his invitation?

ONE

God Saved My Life!

I AM A PSYCHOLOGIST, but nothing in my training or years of clinical practice prepared me for the shock I received that day in the fall of 1972. Barely into my thirties and the father of four small children, I had been examined a few days earlier by a surgeon; and he was calling to report to me the results of a biopsy.

"What's the bad news?" I asked with an attempt at a disarming burst of bravado. He couldn't see the death grip that I had on the telephone receiver.

"It's bad," he replied. "It's melanoma."

What power that word had. Melanoma is one of the deadliest forms of cancer. I remembered that Tom Dooley, a famous missionary physician, had died a heroic death from the same disease while serving the poor and sick in the Third World. But I was not a hero. I had known for the past six months that I had been playing with danger. Though I had the symptoms of cancer, I had denied them. I had simply refused to accept the possibility of that dreaded diagnosis.

The Catholic in me recognized that I had also been playing with another kind of danger. Compromise can be dangerous, and I knew that my lifelong hunger for God and his ways had been seriously compromised. I had grown frustrated with what seemed like a futile search for peace and transformation within Christianity.

While continuing to go to church each Sunday, while clinging to my ancestral Christian faith, I began to search for fresh solutions in Eastern religions. I had become fascinated with Buddhism. Maybe serenity and enlightenment would come to me, as my Zen teachers said, through this new way. The gospel plus Buddha. It proved to be a deadly compromise.

After the surgeon hung up, I told my wife Sally what he had said. We sat by the phone, visibly stunned. Sally is a nurse and psychiatry is her specialty, but what skills could she bring to bear now? Mine is psychology, but I was not trained to face the stark reality of my own death. How were we to deal with the obvious contingencies: Sally's widowhood and our four small children left fatherless?

We had been through hard times before and had known the strength that comes from going through difficulties as a couple. Others saw this strength and came to us with their troubles. But that night we sensed our utter helplessness. We cried and prayed. We didn't sleep at all; instead, we just held hands and prayed through the night.

Zen was no comfort to me in my helplessness. I needed God desperately and I knew it.

The surgeon told me to go to work the next day. He would do his best to hurry someone out of a hospital bed so he could schedule my surgery immediately. He would let Sally know as soon as the arrangements had been made.

I functioned during the first part of that morning like a masterfully programmed robot. I got through the appointments scheduled on my calendar without the clients guessing for a second that I was carrying a lethal secret in my body.

Then the phone call came through. "Marty," Sally said, "the hospital called. You're to be admitted this afternoon. The operation is tomorrow morning. I love you."

Without putting down the receiver, I found myself dialing a man I had never met. He was the respected principal of a large urban elementary school. And his way with students, faculty, and parents was legendary. A drug counselor who had made a remarkable recovery from heroin addiction was the latest person to bring this man to my attention. "What you're searching for, Marty, he has. Give him a call," the counselor told me.

"You don't know me from Adam," I began, "but I need to talk to you." Then I poured out all my anxiety and desperation to this virtual stranger on the other end of the line. He listened and then led me through the most important fifteen minutes of my life. He told me that my needs were all known to God. He explained to me that my long-standing relationship with God was about to come into sharp focus through Jesus' victory over my cancer on the cross.

The word "victory" seared my anxiety-ridden mind and stayed with me. I believed the Scripture this newfound brother read to me. Right there over the phone I met Jesus in a new way. Finally, I confided to this man of faith, who was also a Presbyterian elder, that I wanted to see a Catholic priest before I went to the hospital. "One who believes like you do," I told him.

I sensed that the gift of new life I had experienced through the witness of this new friend in Christ needed to be completed within the practices of my own church. I wanted to receive the Lord's pardon for my sins, which were now as clear as glass before me. I wanted to encounter the merciful Jesus in the sacrament of penance.

For the next leg of my unplanned pilgrimage, my Presbyterian friend directed me to the other side of the city to see the Catholic priest "who believed."

It was early in the afternoon and the rectory was bustling with activity. The priest ushered me through a passageway. Suddenly, we were in the darkened sanctuary of a church.

We sat down on the steps in front of the altar, and I began a remorse-filled confession of my sins. I broke down and cried in front of this total stranger. Yet he had already become my brother in Christ, just like the elementary school principal, my Presbyterian friend. After he extended me forgiveness on behalf of the body of Christ, he asked if I would mind if he prayed over me for healing.

Would I mind! There was nothing I could have preferred!

As he prayed, I knew that Jesus was there at my side. I knew in my heart that he loved me. I knew that he had completely forgiven me! A part of me was saying, "It doesn't even matter if I'm healed. I'll be with him forever." But I couldn't talk out loud at that point, so overwhelmed was I by God's merciful love after I had repented for my sins and received his forgiveness.

Somehow I made my way out of the church and arrived home to pick up Sally, so she could accompany me to the hospital. With her psychiatric expertise, Sally saw my lightheartedness as a desperate attempt to cope. She knew denial to be a classic psychological defense for such a hopeless situation. It was, in fact, the joy of the Lord. The whole hospital admission experience—including the interviews and blood tests—couldn't shake it.

That evening the priest who had prayed with me brought the Eucharist and anointed me with oil for healing. I was bathed in the sweet serenity I had sought for so many years. Shalom. I slept peacefully and prayerfully got ready for surgery the next morning.

At my bedside, I wrote Sally a note telling her that Jesus was with us and that we must trust completely in his love for us. I was even unconcerned enough to offer free advice to the orderly who wheeled me through the hospital corridors to the operating room. He needed to talk about his marriage problems. And I wanted to share the overflow of hope in God I was so profoundly experiencing.

The surgeons were not prepared for what they found. They found nothing. Absolutely nothing! Not a single cancer cell was discovered in the tissue that was removed from my thigh, exposing the muscle and leaving a gaping wound. Because melanoma travels in the blood and the lymphatic system attacking the organs, the eyes, and the brain—they drew what seemed like quarts of blood and rushed it from our own university hospital to the West Coast for exhaustive laboratory analysis.

Again, they found nothing. Absolutely nothing! Where was the deadly melanoma which had threatened to take my life?

Biopsies for four suspicious growths were cancelled. The follow-up surgery to remove my supposedly cancerous lymph nodes was never scheduled. The experimental chemotherapy originally contemplated was never begun. Everything had changed even to the naked eye. And there were no medical explanations!

But I had mine. God had healed me of all traces of an

insidious, incurable disease. *He had saved my life!*

Since the surgery had been performed, I remained in the hospital for two weeks. My leg lay in a cast with a skin graft growing over the exposed muscle where the surgeons had operated.

God had his own ideas about how he wanted me to spend my time. This two-week period found me utterly absorbed in the Bible Sally had packed for me. Day and night I pored over the Scriptures. Sometimes I cried. Sometimes I laughed. Over and over I said, "It's all true. God's Word is all true."

But the nursing staff worried about me. They thought that I might be in some kind of depression because I never opened the blinds to let in daylight! All I did was read the Bible. Sally and I laughed over this compassionate diagnosis. To raise their spirits, I decorated my walls with get-well cards and pictures from our children. I even carved ridiculous faces on two apples and suspended them on strings from rods over my bed.

Then I went back to pouring over the Bible.

Although I had to use crutches and then a cane for several months after surgery, my gait was steady and erect. I was able to see the whole experience of my surgery and convalescence as a clear message from the Lord to me. God wanted to expose and root out the spiritual death that I had stumbled into. He wanted me to walk with him and not to compromise. He wanted me to walk straight without limping, without straggling to the right or to the left. He wanted me healed and whole so that I could live a life of service to my wife, my children, my clients, and to him. He wouldn't settle for less.

One lesson I learned in the weeks immediately after my surgery is that cancer victims suffer a great deal from fear.

The reason for this is obvious: the death toll from this disease is so high that it has come to be dreaded. Even though so many forms of cancer are treatable today—especially if they're discovered early—people are still very fearful when they are diagnosed with any form of cancer.

Because of this high level of fear, the devil often has a field day with cancer patients. He can take advantage of this time of weakness to launch a vicious assault on your faith and inner peace. Family members and friends often don't help matters either. Friends of mine, even medical professionals who really should have known better, would walk up to me and say something like, "You look so good! No one would suspect that you're dealing with cancer."

Cancer patients and people diagnosed with other serious diseases should expect that these kinds of things will happen and be prepared to deal with them. The only way I could deal with them was to turn to the Lord and ask him to give me the strength, the faith, and the peace that I needed. And he did every time. I discovered that I could depend upon God for my healing. I believe that he will do the same for others who suffer from the effects of a serious illness. The Lord is there for all who call upon him and his saving power.

Restored and saved by the Lord, I could proclaim, "The living, the living are the ones who give you thanks, as I do today. Fathers declare to their sons, O God, your faithfulness" (Is 38:19). That passage from Isaiah became something of a motto for me for several years after God had healed me. Even today, fifteen years later, I have not forgotten what God did for me and my family. Every day Sally and I declare to our sons, our daughter, and to anyone who will listen: "God is faithful. God heals."

"*I Knew God Would Heal My Husband*"

The day that Martin was admitted to the hospital was a very trying day for me. I had to make a number of arrangements for the care of our four children. Then I accompanied my husband through the tedious procedures for hospital admissions. Finally, all the necessary paperwork and medical tests were behind us. I sat next to Martin's bed trying to act very cheerful when I was actually very frightened.

My experience in nursing left me little hope. I knew melanoma was nearly always fatal. I had also recently grieved over the deaths of my father and my brother. These things preoccupied me as I kissed my husband good night and walked out of the hospital.

I was almost in tears by the time I arrived at the car for the drive home.

Then something wonderful happened. I got in the car, composed myself, and simply asked the Lord to heal my husband. "I love Martin," I told God. "I don't want him to die. I will give you my life if you will spare his."

Immediately, I sensed the presence of Jesus. I had never had that kind of a spiritual experience before. But I knew it came from God. I was keenly aware of his presence as I started the car and drove home.

The image of Jesus remained fixed before my eyes from the hospital parking lot to my driveway, a distance of ten miles! What I sensed was a deep peace and security that came from knowing Jesus was with me.

I knew then that he loved Martin and me. And somehow I knew that he was going to drive the cancer from my husband's body. Jesus' reassuring countenance and his committed love for both of us made it clear to me that this was a time of new beginnings and a time for honoring promises. Little did I know how true that spiritual sense would prove to be.

As I look back on that night, I am amazed that I did not allow my psychiatric training to take over and make me deny that spiritual experience. As a professional, I should have diagnosed my experience as a hallucination. I should have concluded that I had fabricated a delusion out of desperation. My husband was dying, after all. Excessive self-protection in the form of a delusion would have been quite understandable.

Yet God broke through. I did not doubt his love and his word. I received a special gift of faith that night. God had taken me up on my offer to give my life to him!

After I arrived home, I checked on my children. Then I sat down and prayed far into the night.

God heard my prayers. The next day we discovered the miracle that had the surgeons baffled!

That very night the Lord also began to reach down inside of me to heal a frightened and wounded little girl. Was it possible? God could heal my husband of a deadly disease. But could he heal me of the deep emotional trauma of years of emotional abuse and rejection? Could he?

TWO

An Abused Child Made Whole

Can a mother forget her infant, be without tenderness for the child of her womb? Even should she forget, I will never forget you. (Is 49:15)

FALLING, FALLING DOWN A LONG and winding staircase until finally—once again—I experience a painful thump at the bottom of the stairs and wake up from a fitful sleep. I try to settle down, hoping not to be awakened again tonight in the same dreaded way.

Many people have come to Martin and me complaining of terrifying nightmares or dreams similar to this one. We invariably discover they're related to foundational insecurities in a person's life which began in infancy because of abuse and neglect by parents. Such insecurities always strike at the very core of a person's sense of self and leave nagging doubts of worthlessness. The deserted infant or toddler buried deep inside us cries out, "Do I have any right to be alive?"

In my case, this frightening dream of falling down a staircase recurred every night for nearly thirty-five years. What foundational insecurity had held me bound for so long? I hoped against hope that the Lord would heal me quickly of this nightly trauma after Martin's own miraculous deliverance from cancer.

Yet in his wisdom, God chose to reveal and heal other deep-seated traumas first, such as the intense guilt and grief I experienced after my brother Bob's tragic death. The Lord knew best when and how to heal the frightened and wounded little girl deep inside of me.

On a crisp spring night in April of 1969, I received the devastating phone call about Bob. I was informed that my poor, troubled brother had committed suicide by jumping out of a sixth-story window at a Chicago hotel. And he was barely twenty-nine years old. His suicide occurred just six months after the death of my father, causing me intense grief and guilt.

Bob and I had had an unusually close brother-sister relationship growing up. We were the two older children in our family, separated by only a year and a half. And we both faced rejection and abuse during childhood.

Sadly, Bob never recovered from the deep emotional traumas he suffered in his early years. After our marriage, Martin and I made numerous attempts to get Bob the psychiatric help he so desperately needed. But he didn't seem capable of deciding to accept our help. You can imagine my grief and guilt after his suicide.

I told myself that I should have been more available to him and more insistent that he get help. I should have created a scene at the hospital the night the psychiatric resident refused to admit Bob, despite his immediate suicide attempt and history of psychiatric illness.

Bob left that emergency room, got on a train to Chicago, and found his way out of nearly three decades of pain.

You can imagine the recriminations. I suffered so intensely from nightmares that I could hardly sleep at all. This draining preoccupation did not progress to the point where I needed professional help myself. But day after day I recalled Bob's suicide, and the pain took its toll. It left scars deep inside of me that continued to fester for years.

Even though I didn't have a close personal relationship with God then, he blessed me with a wonderful gift during that difficult period of grieving. We had three boys and I had become pregnant with our fourth child shortly before my father's death. Just imagine my joy when our little girl, Claire, was born just two weeks before my brother's death. The joy of this new life, my precious daughter, helped me cope with the emotional trauma over the losses of my father and my brother.

Then during the Christmas season several years later, God blessed me with another remarkable gift. A priest who is a childhood friend of mine dropped in for a holiday visit. He had just recently been baptized in the Holy Spirit and had been on a healing retreat with Agnes Sanford. He knew about the emotional pain and grief I had been carrying since my brother's suicide and asked if he could pray with me.

I agreed. And he prayed a very simple prayer from the heart, asking the Lord to be with me.

I experienced instant release! The holiness of Jesus and his divine mercy flooded me with joy. Immediately, I had a deep assurance that my traumatized brother had encountered the Lord at the instant of his violent death. All at once I felt that Bob's wounded soul had tasted of this divine mercy. I felt he had received the opportunity to make a declaration of faith in Jesus as his savior, even as he plummeted to his death from the sixth-story window of that Chicago hotel back in 1969. Of course, I can't prove that what I sensed spiritually about Bob actually happened. But I did have a strong sense that God was comforting me.

The memory of Bob's suicide still brings sadness to my heart because of my great love for him. But the Lord has neutralized that memory's power to rob me of his peace and joy. Now I can think about Bob's death without nagging guilt. I can rejoice in our relationship as loving siblings who, I believe, have met their merciful savior.

That emotional and spiritual release in the Holy Spirit was a powerful liberation for me. I felt like a new creation in Christ. Little did I know, though, that God had only begun to touch my life. The deep foundational healing I so desperately needed was yet to come.

It happened sometime later right out of the blue while I was deep in prayer one day. In my mind's eye, I saw the distinct image of a young, pregnant woman throwing herself down a long and winding staircase in a desperate attempt to abort the life within her. It was the staircase in my nightmare.

To my shock and horror, that woman was unmistakably my mother! She was pregnant with me. And in her distress, she was trying to kill me!

I now understood the terrible meaning of my dreaded nightmare in a flash of intuition. But God was merciful. The horrible scene didn't end there. As I saw the tortured body of my mother strike the floor at the bottom of the stairway, the hands of my loving Lord were poised to catch the terrified baby in her womb. The Lord was safeguarding my life for service in his kingdom.

I began to understand and experience a blessed release.

From that moment, the nightmares ceased and have never returned. God also gave me the grace to forgive my mother without any reservations.

At just the right moment, without any fanfare, God had given me sweet liberty from that deep-seated trauma. He knew the moment when I would be able to receive that life-changing revelation and was there with his love. What sweet liberty!

Forgiveness proved to be the key to my inner healing from that foundational insecurity of parental abuse and neglect. I began to understand how important forgiveness is in the lives of individuals and the whole human race. If God had not been willing to forgive us, even when we had not humbly asked him for mercy, Jesus could not have come. And if Jesus had not come, healing and restoration would not have been possible for me and countless others. Mercy. Compassion. Reconciliation. These profound fruits of Jesus' victory on Calvary were now able to come into my life and bring deep, cleansing inner healing.

I began to understand why even small disagreements with my husband over the years had produced tremendous bouts of anxiety. Even an abrupt word from him would sometimes activate a whirl of thoughts and feelings that made it seem like my world was falling apart. Surely, I would think, the beautiful life and the wonderful family I had could not last.

But that special day when the Lord showed me the scene of my prenatal rejection, I began to understand the affirming and life-giving love of my saving Lord. He supplied me with the truth and spiritual insight that set me free. He gave me comprehension that went beyond ordinary insight.

With divine compassion as my guide and my critical judgement suspended, I knew that my mother had done the best she could. I understood in a completely new way her own foundational insecurities. They were also the legacy of a troubled childhood. The third of four daughters born to a prosperous executive whose work came before his family, she found herself competing for his affirmation. The competition was fierce right up to the time of my grandfather's death when he was in his eighties. In fact, bitter rivalry involving the four sisters and their widowed mother persisted right up to the time of grandma's death a few years ago.

This kind of an upbringing really did not prepare her for the give-and-take of marriage and child rearing. The financially insecure situation in which she and her twenty-year-old bridegroom launched their marriage further complicated matters. Barely out of his teens with no developed career or nest egg, her young bridegroom was dependent upon his new father-in-law for employment in the family company. Yet there had already been strain on both sides of the family before the couple even exchanged vows.

I realized how deeply disappointed my mother had been when her first pregnancy produced a boy. A little girl herself emotionally, she had counted on a baby girl to fulfill her dreams of frilly doll play with the idealized daughter she had always wanted to be.

After my brother Bob's birth, my mother became upset and estranged from my father emotionally. They even separated for a time. But their eventual reconciliation didn't succeed. Its immediate by-product was yet another pregnancy, which brought me into the world. This pregnancy was an emotional blow my mother just couldn't absorb.

She became desperate. Her attempt at self-induced abortion failed. And her poisoned feelings at that time may have contributed to the disordered metabolism that caused toxins to circulate in her bloodstream. Toxemia kept her bedridden in the hospital for two months.

Then her little girl was born. How sad after all of the struggle that the baby girl she had wanted was now a living symbol of all the pain in her life! It didn't take long for the little girl to become Momma's archrival by charming Daddy and her grandparents. And the little girl knew it. Early in life she knew the tightening grip of maternal hostility. How early it was I can't recall, but at some moment—at some core place deep inside of me—I perceived that I was a source of distress to my mother.

I began to catch myself in front of my father, being careful to control my responses to his affection so that I did not upset my mother. I tried to earn her love throughout my childhood by doing a lot of housework and by saving up my change to buy her presents. Later, I would even save up my money to take her out to lunch.

Nothing worked. My mother resented me and I was unable to change that tragic fact. The rejection and hostility increased during my teenage years and peaked on what should have been two of the happiest days in both of our lives. First, as class valedictorian at my elementary school graduation, I had to explain why my mother—though quite well—would not attend.

As predictable as it might have been, how much more painful was it for me years later at my wedding. I had to explain to my bridegroom's consoling family that my mother wouldn't be attending our wedding. In fact, she wouldn't allow any of my family to come and celebrate with me on one of the happiest days of my life. She even went to great lengths to discourage anyone she could from attending our wedding, so deeply had she come to resent me.

Yet God in his infinite mercy has healed me and given me the grace to forgive my mother. The knowledge of that remarkable healing at the hands of my loving Father has given me the compassion and confidence to pass along God's mercy through counsel and prayer with others for inner healing.

As I've prayed about my own deep inner healing and seen God heal foundational insecurities in others, the Lord has given me a valuable insight. Our earthly parents—as important as they may seem—are really something of a bonus. Some people have good parents, and they are truly blessed. But even if parents fail, each child still has recourse to the ultimate parent: God our Father who is in heaven.

Our earthly parents' main task is really to introduce us to our Father, the one who has unalterable love for each one of his sons and daughters.

This profound truth has revolutionized my life. I've learned that God my Father loves me because he has gone out of his way to save me and to heal me. In his incredible mercy, he has saved me and set me free through the sacrifice of his Son Jesus. That love for me will stand forever. And I long to share the Father's unconditional love with all of my brothers and sisters, all of his sons and daughters.

God my Father in his wisdom also knew that I needed a mother. My own mother had abused and rejected me, so the Father gave me a precious gift through his Son. He gave me Mary, the mother of Jesus, as my own spiritual mother.

Within the first month of my being baptized in the Holy Spirit, the beautiful lady made her appearance into my life. Martin was in the surgeon's office for further scrutiny to check for melanoma. The skin graft had been taking and was steadily covering the gaping wound on his thigh where the surgeons had removed the tissue right down to the muscle to check for the deadly cancer.

Imagine our alarm when we saw that several frightening blue lesions had erupted on the new skin covering the thigh muscle. That night, Martin was lying in bed unable to sleep, worry etched on his face. I was at his side praying in the Spirit.

Suddenly, I sensed Mary's presence as she joined me in interceding for my husband. Though unexpected and unsolicited, she had come. I found myself being washed in an experience of maternal love that moved me to tears of joy and collaborative intercession. At last, here was a mother who would stand by me. Here was a mother who would love me unconditionally.

Martin, for his part, grew peaceful and still. As he drifted off to sleep, he said, "I feel a vibration in my leg. A little noise like an electric motor buzzing."

The next morning we saw the results of the strange buzzing. It was the handiwork of that marvelous time of intercession. Martin's condition had miraculously improved overnight. There were no more lesions! The skin graft was clearer and healthier than ever.

Jesus had introduced me to his mother, and he had certainly gotten my attention. Yet I'm a convert to Roman Catholicism and still had many questions about Mary's role at that time. Just imagine my amazement!

In fact, a few months later, I began to sense her intercession again at charismatic prayer meetings we were hosting for college students at our home. In this interdenominational gathering of young people who were learning to say "no" to the world and "yes" to Jesus, she came as an intercessor. This time she came as a mother to intercede for the youth, as if in mourning over the actual and potential loss of so many of that generation.

Her quiet and hidden presence at those meetings filled me with deep consolation. I experienced firsthand her special role as our spiritual mother and a mighty intercessor for God's people. I knew that she was the mother of the Lord. But I now understood why Jesus had given her to my brothers and sisters and me. We needed a spiritual mother.

What a powerful healing for me! After so much hurt and rejection at the hands of my own mother, Jesus had given me Mary as my own dear mother. Here was a mother whose example I could follow. I knew she would teach me to honor God by the way of obedience, the way of quietness, and the way of littleness.

God was healing me and bringing me to himself. He was beginning to reveal to me that healing, properly understood, is a grace for holiness and conversion. Like the Samaritan who was healed of leprosy, I felt immense gratitude and awe in the presence of the holy one who had healed me as my loving Father.

God Healed Our Family and Gave Us a Ministry

The immediate effects on our marriage and our family were almost as profound as the wonderful changes God wrought in both of us. As a married couple and a family, we learned how to practice agape love in our daily lives. We began to see that this kind of "lived-out" committed love for each other is absolutely essential for the affirmation and consolidation of inner healing.

After all, healing is an act of love from an all-holy God to one of his sons and daughters. The purpose is to draw us into a closer relationship of love with him and each other. God wants to launch us on a lifetime of cooperation with his mercy-filled grace, so he can release agape love into our midst. Yes, healed people are meant to be shining images of God's love and truth in a world that too many times settles for hollow counterfeits of the real thing. For us, this meant that God wanted to transform our relationships as a married couple and a family. It also meant he wanted us to go out and share the good news of healing and conversion with a broken and wounded world.

We experienced a particularly poignant example of this in our family life. Relationships in our nuclear family had always been unusually close and harmonious. Now even the little teasings between siblings began to yield to a higher principle of charity and mercy. Our third son John, closest in age to our baby and only daughter Claire, acted out a heroic expression of brotherly love that we will never forget.

It was late in August and we were enjoying a day on the beach off the coast of Maine. At that time, John and Claire were inclined to experience sparks of conflict in their relationship. We were vacationing and the children were on sturdy rafts, exploring the coves and rocks that studded the peaceful inlet of John's Bay across from Christmas Cove.

Suddenly, the deep, still waters turned violent as a wild storm whipped its way into the little harbor. Claire's raft struck a rock and started to deflate. She managed to grab ahold of the rock and perch herself on its wet and mossy back as wave upon wave battered her.

John and Marty Jr. miraculously made their way through the choppy waves to the rock in a two-man raft. John quickly clambered up onto the slippery rock and gave up his place of safety in the raft to Claire. He took her place on the rock, waiting for the help that we quickly summoned from the shore.

There was no way to swim in the pounding surf amidst the treacherous rocks of the cove, so we could only wait. By another miracle, Marty and Claire made it safely to shore in the two-man raft. And after a very close call, John was rescued with the help of a good samaritan's boat.

As John emerged from the surf, his bloody legs gave testimony to the depths of the love that had transformed a relationship best described as an uneasy truce into one that had called forth heroism. To this day, the entire family remembers "Prayer Rock" with vivid detail and great thanksgiving.

God also showed us that we needed to stand in faith as a married couple and a family. We needed to rely on his word and his promises. We learned the important principle that our faith paved the way for God to work in power.

We see this key truth constantly at work in Scripture. For example, in Matthew the Evangelist's account of Jesus healing two blind men, the Lord asks the men, "'Are you confident I can do this?' 'Yes, Lord,' they told him. At that he touched their eyes and said, 'Because of your faith it shall be done to you'; And they recovered their sight" (Mt 9:28-30).

We need to believe in our hearts that the Lord has the ability and the desire to heal us. Once we have that kind of faith planted in our hearts and minds, God can and will act. Just as he did in New Testament times, just as he has in our lives, God will act in the life of anyone who puts his trust in his saving power.

My healing as a sister and a daughter and then the "working out" of that healing as a wife and mother were all part of God's master plan of transformation for each member of our family. What we saw happening under our own roof gave us confidence to put our professional training and our whole lives at the Lord's disposal.

I began to realize that my clinical and teaching background as a psychiatric nurse was a valuable asset as I stepped out in faith and love to help an increasing stream of people who came to us for counseling. They came with stories of abuse and neglect. They came with stories of other forms of crippling psychological trauma.

Before my spiritual awakening, it was common for disturbed patients and troubled souls to gravitate to me on the grounds or in the cafeteria of the large psychiatric hospital where I taught and did clinical work. They could sense a receptivity and a compassion in me. My co-workers even used to kid me about it. How much more natural, then, for the same sort of thing to happen even more when God's grace for healing began operating freely in our lives. Of course, Martin and I couldn't hide the real source and purpose behind our gifts for counseling: the Lord Jesus and his saving, healing grace.

We had seen God work powerfully through inner

healing in our marriage, our family, and ourselves. But it wasn't until a young man named John entered our lives that we had a sure conviction about the spiritual purposes of inner healing.

It was hard to believe that John's incredible story of abuse and neglect was true. Was this capable and loving young man really the same person? What was the Lord trying to teach us?

THREE

A Grace for Holiness

A FEW MONTHS BEFORE JOHN was born his father deserted the family, leaving his pregnant wife in total disgrace. In Burma, custom dictated that a fatherless boy be placed for adoption. John was adopted by a Muslim family. When he was six years old, John was enrolled in the rites that were to lead to his full initiation into Islam.

When word of this reached his biological grandmother, she was outraged. In her view despite the disgrace of his birth John was born to be a Buddhist. In fact, his natural mother was a Buddhist priestess of high rank. Rather than allow the occurrence of what she considered to be a religious abomination, John's grandmother went to the great expense of purchasing the boy back from his adoptive parents.

It was a traumatic experience for this six-year-old who had been given up at birth and had lived with another family during his early years. He was suddenly sold to an old woman he had never so much as laid eyes on.

Later, as John was finally recovering from his distress and submitting to the ways of his new, though original, Buddhist family—he began to hear a call from the God of the Christians. He could no longer stifle the insistent call from the Lord as his eighteenth birthday approached. He became a Christian. His natural family considered this to be the ultimate blasphemy and they shunned him. He was cast out of the family, and all those he loved considered him to be dead.

Despite the great personal cost, John persisted in his walk with Jesus Christ. He joined the Roman Catholic Church and became active in spiritual renewal. I met him nine years later when he was representing his country at an international conference of Catholic charismatic renewal leaders in Rome. By this time John was a strong, vibrant man of God. He had travelled a very hard road, but he had come through it.

Despite the absence of family ties, John had come to realize that the only lasting security any one of us can really attain is the unshakable love of our heavenly Father. What an inner healing that was for this young man. And he had come to this insight and to his committed response without the benefit of counseling sessions and prayer ministry!

Though his family had given him up as dead, John had never given up on them. He had been unable to maintain contact with them, but he had faithfully kept them in his prayers. Just three months before our conference John received word that his mother had also heard a call from the God of the Christians and had been baptized into the church. What a wonderful day it was for that faithful son! He was reunited with his mother and together they began praying for the rest of the family.

John's story is a moving and remarkable example of God healing grave psychological traumas that some experience as children. More than that it is a powerful testimony that God can sovereignly heal deeply rooted foundational insecurities when we turn to him in faith.

The key we began to see in John's life and in our own had been wholehearted conversion to God as we responded to his saving and healing grace. It wasn't primarily a matter of a special technique such as imaging past hurts for healing of the memories and then bringing Jesus into those painful situations. Such techniques typically have a place in an inner healing ministry. But it was John's response to grace and our response to grace that proved decisive.

Moreover, we saw that John's healing—just like ours—had enabled God to use him as an instrument for healing in the lives of others. God used this restored young man to bring spiritual restoration to his natural mother, one of the principal figures who had hurt him so profoundly. For us, John's story was full of lessons about forgiveness, perseverance, and love of one's enemies. God used all of these things to bring John to the fullness of life which, in turn, led to freedom for his mother and then many others through his work in spiritual renewal. We were reminded of God transforming our own marriage and family and then calling us to minister to our clients in the area of inner healing.

Through John's inspiring example and many more over the years, we became convinced that God was calling us to accept inner healing as a grace for holiness and conversion in our ministry to others. We weren't to rely primarily on a repertoire of techniques or a pat format for counseling sessions. We wanted to apply our professional training and our spiritual gifts. But it became clear that the crucial point in any healing had to be each individual's response to God's grace. Our task was to use the skills God had given us to sensitively and prayerfully get our clients to the place where they could receive God's grace for wholeness and holiness. All aspects of our healing ministry had to serve that overriding purpose.

Even as God began blessing us with this sure focus on his healing grace, he also issued an exciting and challenging call to us as Christian therapists. We were led to seek out fellowship and professional collaboration with other Christian therapists involved in the healing ministry. This informal sharing of views and insights eventually led to our involvement in the founding of the Association of Christian Therapists in 1975.

A vision for the association came together at a conference attended by twenty-five health-care professionals in 1975 on Staten Island in New York City. Each of us had experienced the healing touch of the Lord. That week-long conference changed our lives even more. Listening to one another's faith stories drawn from the healing ministry led us into deeper times of fellowship and prayer. United in deep prayer, we heard the Lord speak to us about claiming our professions for Jesus Christ.

God gave us a truly exciting vision of combining our faith in him with our professional training in caring for suffering people. And we could stand together and share our resources in this common mission as Christian therapists. Thus, ACT was born.

In 1985, as ACT celebrated its tenth birthday, the association had grown to more than two thousand members. Some of the members were well-known names in the ministry of healing. But the majority of the membership consisted of ordinary doctors, nurses, psychologists, counselors, and other health-care professionals. Priests, religious sisters, and lay people involved in healing ministries had also joined us.

ACT's purpose was not to create new healing ministries. Our call was to help well-known and ordinary Christians alike extend God's grace for healing to others in ways that would be both effective and faithful to the scriptural presentation of healing as the herald of evangelization. For instance, in the Acts of the Apostles, the early Christian community in Jerusalem prays, "Grant to your servants, even as they speak your words, complete assurance by stretching forth your hand in cures and signs and wonders to be worked in the name of Jesus, your holy Servant" (Acts 4:29-30).

Here is healing in its proper perspective. The power of God to heal is simply one of the mighty signs and wonders that are provided as helps to conversion. Healing isn't an end in itself. It is a confirming herald for evangelization, a sign of the kingdom of God as a manifestation of his power and glory. It calls the healed one to live the rest of his life for God.

Although from the beginning ACT had been open to men and women from all Christian backgrounds, the vast majority of its members have been Catholics who have experienced conversion through the charismatic renewal or some other renewal movement. The influence of an awakened, deepened Roman Catholic spirituality in ACT fostered an atmosphere of warm hospitality to brothers and sisters of all Christian churches, while also supporting the organization's identity as a Catholic group. Because of this strong sense of identity, ACT proved to be a very effective and rewarding fellowship for Christian therapists and healers, growing steadily over its first ten years.

During its first four years, the association operated out of borrowed hospital facilities in Toledo, Ohio. Then in

1979, the board of directors asked us to become the organization's executive co-directors. ACT's headquarters were located in our hometown of Rochester, New York, from then until the summer of 1986.

We devoted a great deal of time and energy to its development. Under the anointing of the Spirit, we were able to contribute to the growth of the association. Our vision for ACT was that it should develop a stable, fully scriptural approach to "wholeness and holiness" during a time of great confusion and syncretism in the area of healing. As our motto read, "Toward wholeness and holiness through prayer in the healing professions."

The Lord gave us sobering insights into our responsibility to foster the formation of a *holy* people and not just a *healed* people. That responsibility began clearly with ourselves as the co-directors and with our members as ministers of healing.

A holy king wants holy servants. Our doctors, nurses, psychotherapists, and charismatic healers were to see their place in healing within the larger context of building God's holy kingdom with "living stones."

During the summer of 1986, ACT's board of directors decided that they wanted to take a fresh look at the organization's direction and mission. We agreed to step aside as the association's executive co-directors to let other ACT members lead the way. It proved a painful separation for us—any such separation always is—and we found we had to withdraw from ACT altogether.

We sought the Lord's will for our lives during the summer and fall of 1986. Our conviction grew that God intended us to continue in the healing ministry. We also sensed his call to continue communicating the vision for healing that the Lord had given us during our years as leaders of ACT.

Furthermore, God seemed to be calling us to help form a new generation of young Christian leaders—many of whom would resonate with the mission to raise up a holy people to serve a holy king through the right balance of prayer and study of the behavioral sciences. This led us in 1987 to accept an invitation to join the exciting work of the Franciscan University of Steubenville in Ohio.

In the eight-hundred-year tradition of Francis of Assisi, the Franciscan University of Steubenville sees its mission as the rebuilding of the church by forming living stones of all ages. A growing Christian outreach center presents summer conferences. The Catholic Evangelization Training School teaches both clergy and lay Catholics how to better spread the gospel. Students are trained in twenty-nine fields of study within an environment of Christian faith.

From our new base in Steubenville, we continue to teach what we've learned to be a foundational truth of human life: namely, that God desires to make his people whole and holy. Our experience during fifteen years of healing ministry is that wholeness and holiness are essential for everyone.

Our heavenly Father wants to break through into every human life where distress and ill health threaten mental and physical wholeness. Healing is not just for some chosen few. Living radical lives for God is not just for so-called "religious fanatics." Jesus shed his blood for one and all, so that every human being could have access to eternal life in heaven and abundant life here on earth.

During our fifteen years of ministry, what are some of

the important principles God has taught us about inner healing? What are the life-changing principles of the kingdom that have made a difference in the lives of our clients?

One important life-changing principle has been the truth in love.

The ways of the Lord are mysterious. But the essence of all of his mysterious interventions in our lives is always this: love-in-truth; truth-in-love. Never just love. Never just truth.

Love without truth is a sugary illusion at best. It is like trying to satisfy hunger pangs by munching on a cone of cotton candy—nothing more than a spoonful of sugar spun out with air just can't satisfy our gnawing hunger. Truth without love, on the other hand, is merciless. But when we confront the truth about ourselves and respond to God's grace, we come face to face with his love and mercy. We are set free.

Facing the truth in love for Arthur didn't come easily. But it proved to be a matter of life and death.

Arthur was dying of cancer, but his problems were much more serious than mere physical illness. Could he accept the truth in love? Could he see past the physical pain to the more serious problems of the heart and the soul?

FOUR

God Wants His
People Whole

ARTHUR WAS VERY SICK when he came forward and asked for prayer during a time of ministry at an area church. He was dying of cancer. An elderly man, Arthur's prayer was that God would heal him and prolong his life. He was surrounded by his entire family: his wife, his adult children, and several grandchildren. We were deeply moved at the sight of this large family begging God to spare Arthur's life. We prayed mightily that night.

Several months later Arthur came to see us. God had healed him and taken away the cancer. But something even more important had happened. God had delivered him from the destructive vices of alcoholism, drug addiction, and compulsive gambling.

"I didn't want to go to that healing service," he told us. "My children practically dragged me there. But I'm glad I went. My real problem was not the cancer. It was the other things—the alcoholism, drug abuse, and gambling," he explained.

"I had so many vices for so long that a lot of damage had been done to every member of my family. When God began to touch my body as you prayed, all the truth about my lifestyle flashed before me. I could feel his love, and I knew what had to happen.

"I felt a new hope because the compulsions lifted. That made it possible for the family to work out all the relationship problems that had developed over the years. The prayers you said over me that night made it possible for love to grow in my family again," he concluded.

Arthur had confronted the truth in love and discovered the true meaning of freedom. God was able to minister physical and spiritual healing to him as he confronted his sin and repented. God's healing love enveloped him, and the blessings spilled over into the life of his family—a family that had formerly been damaged by the serious sin in his life. We were reminded of how Martin had confronted his own deadly compromise of the gospel plus Buddha and then repented before his miraculous healing from melanoma.

What God did for Arthur helped us understand better the concept of true wholeness. There can be no doubt that the Lord wants us to be well in every way. But the aim of wholeness is not just personal well-being and self-fulfillment. God's intention in inner healing is to enable us to love him and our neighbor in ever deeper ways.

Just as St. Paul wrote to the Corinthians in his discussion on spiritual gifts, the gifts are helpful, he tells us. They are essential to the growth of the church. But their purpose is to express love in tangible ways. The apostle admonishes us to "seek eagerly after love" (1 Cor 14:1). This applies as much to inner healing and the quest for wholeness as it does to the exercise of spiritual gifts or other areas of spiritual growth.

This truth was played out in Arthur's life in a very interesting way. About a year after all the symptoms of cancer had disappeared, the disease reappeared in another part of his body. And he died within a few months. Although Arthur was dead, his soul had been reclaimed by God. Also his family now lived with happy memories of his conversion and their reconciliation with him. Had Arthur died without inner healing, he may well have left a legacy of bitter memories behind instead.

As we reflected on Arthur's case and others like it, we concluded that healing doesn't occur in a vacuum. God is not like a doctor who prescribes sedatives for us when we get an occasional migraine headache. To the contrary, he wants to bring lasting wholeness, forgiveness, reconciliation, and blessed mercy to the afflicted person and to all of his relationships.

Most of our experiences as Christian therapists in counseling have been devoted to people with emotional and mental disorders who are seeking healing. Tragically, the wholeness that God wants for every person eludes many of those with such disorders, even those who are committed Christians. This is why releasing the full potential of inner healing into disordered lives is so important. It can make a significant lifelong difference.

What are some of these emotional and mental disorders?

There are many ailments that professionals in mental health describe as disturbances. In almost every case, such disturbances can best be understood as things that disturb God's perfect plan for his creature's wholeness. By this we mean the harmony of mind, body, and spirit when all three are infused with the knowledge of God's love.

We believe this is the case with the story of the Samaritan woman whom Jesus encounters at Jacob's well in the Gospel of John (see Jn 4:4-42). The woman has been married a number of times. The man she is presently living with is not her husband. And she tries to hide her sin from Jesus.

Jesus discerns her desperate need to hear the truth in love, so she can be made whole. After being confronted with the truth, she is so moved that she rushes back into town and gives testimony on Jesus' behalf.

"He told me everything I ever did," she confesses (Jn 4:39).

Her persuasive testimony causes many in her town to turn to Jesus. But each one must come to a personal faith in Jesus, just as she had. "No longer does our faith depend on your story," the townspeople tell her after meeting the Lord themselves. "We have heard for ourselves, and we know that this really is the Savior of the world" (Jn 4:42).

John the Evangelist does not tell us that the Samaritan woman is healed of a disorder that had caused her to seek relations with different men. Nor does he tell us that she repented and restored the relationships her sinful behavior had damaged. These things are left for us to infer. But it is clear that due to her encounter with the Lord the woman recognizes Jesus as the one who can heal and restore her. Also, she cannot resist healing's herald call: she becomes an evangelizer by sharing the good news of what Jesus has done for her.

Not all disturbances are as radical as that of the Samaritan woman, but many are. They seriously jeopardize God's plan for one of his children, often starting in infancy or early childhood. Sally's story is a good example of this kind of foundational disturbance or insecurity. In fact, her disturbance started even before birth.

Usually such foundational assaults on a child leave

devastating effects that need to be resolved later in life with professional help. Unfortunately, secular therapy can rarely provide a lasting cure for these kinds of disturbances. People who suffer from them either become chronic psychiatric patients, or they drop out of therapy and wreak havoc on the mental health of those around them, especially their spouses and children.

Christians suffering from foundational disturbances do not have to settle for inadequate secular solutions. Through the ministry of inner healing—which combines prayer and Christian counseling with professional care—many people have been freed from foundational disturbances much the way Sally was freed. Inner healing is part of God's provision for wholeness for those suffering from such disturbances. It is also part of God's provision for those suffering from less acute but nonetheless painful ailments we'll call distresses.

Distresses have their roots during less fragile times in a person's life than foundational disturbances. Perhaps the person was subjected to emotional trauma by a dog attack as a toddler or by a sexual attack as an adolescent. Distresses may not always carry the lifelong consequences of disturbances, but they are real impediments to God's perfect plan for a peaceful, joyful Christian life. Distresses also offer the person seeking help an opportunity for receiving healing grace.

There are times when inner healing can prove helpful even for those who seem emotionally quite healthy. God wants each of us to learn in as many ways and as deeply as possible what wholeness really means. Often the most "together" of us—those with the greatest resilience to life's bumps and bruises—are less whole than we would care to admit. No one is completely whole in any aspect of human life. We are all subject to so many negative, limiting, hurtful influences because of the evil that abounds in the world. But God can break through and heal when we ask in faith and seek qualified help.

A good example of God's power being manifest in inner healing in the life of a seemingly healthy person is the case of Matt. Matt was a successful businessman. He had had a long, happy marriage and had raised two now happily married daughters. He had what he described as a perfect family and he had gone through life without any serious problems. It was a wonderful life, but one that left him totally unprepared for what had happened five months before he came to the office to talk to Martin about his distress.

When we first saw Matt he was almost completely immobilized by a deep depression. It was hard to believe what his wife had told us: that for all of his sixty-four years Matt had been a vigorous and jovial man. He had, she said, decided to take early retirement several months before and had set up an impressive daily schedule for himself that guaranteed that this would not be a rocking-chair retirement. Yet he had turned away from all of this and spent most of his time in isolation, crying inconsolably. He was unable to sleep. He simply wanted to die.

The cause of this crippling depression was anger. Matt was angry with himself because he had not prevented his daughter from taking his only grandson on the car trip that was to result in the boy's death. He was angry with everyone connected in any way with the accident. Most significantly, Matt was furious with God for "taking his grandson."

"Mark was more a son than a grandson," Matt sobbed during that first visit to our office. "He was the son I never had. He was a natural athlete, a born leader. He was handsome, courteous, cheerful, helpful. Everyone loved him, but no one loved him like I did.

"He made my day, every day. 'Gramps,' he would say, 'let's go play some miniature golf,' or 'let's go get a pizza, just you and me.' I can hear him now. I can see him now. But I can't touch him ever again. I can't love him. He was only nine years old. Why did God do this to me?"

Although the boy had been dead for six months, Matt was unable to let go of his grandson. The rest of the family had appropriately mourned and wept. They had buried this wonderful youngster and had dealt with the tremendous grief exhibited by the boy's bewildered classmates at his funeral. Mark's mother and sister, both of whom had survived the crash, had come to terms with what had happened and were already carrying on with their lives. For the rest of the family Mark was gone. But not for Gramps.

The first thing we did was to encourage Matt to express his feelings. With this encouragement he expressed his anger with his daughter, with God, and with himself. He was even angry with Mark, whose abrupt departure from this life had hurt him so. After the anger was released, Matt was able to pause and pray. We asked the Holy Spirit to enlighten us about how we should deal with the frustration and despair that weighed heavily on Matt's heart.

Matt told us that he was a lifelong, churchgoing man. He believed in God, in his power, and in eternal life. But his personal knowledge of Jesus and his experience of the Holy Spirit were not well developed. As Martin listened for guidance from the Holy Spirit, he sensed that Matt needed to experience the love of God the Father in a new way. He needed to experience in his own life the fruit of the perfect father-son relationship that exists between the Father and Jesus. Martin sensed that when he experienced this relationship Matt would understand the vital importance of sacrifice in any love relationship.

Matt also needed to receive the Holy Spirit into his life. He needed to discover how the love which is generated from the love between the Father and Jesus is the Spirit of divine grace, the Spirit of divine power, the Holy Spirit.

We explained these things to Matt and then prayed. The Holy Spirit provided the words, and the words stirred up images and emotions that Matt simply could not resist. With newly opened spiritual eyes, he saw the Father and experienced his love. He saw Jesus, the perfect son. He came in touch with Jesus' sacrificial death, the perfect response to the world's great need, the source of healing for Matt's own grief.

Then he experienced the reality of the Holy Spirit, the Spirit of truth-in-love, the mercy-bearer who brought the required grace, so Matt could face his sense of loss and grief. Through these images and experiences, God showed Matt and us what needed to happen next in order for divine grace to accomplish its work.

Without contrivance, Matt saw another picture, clear and inviting. Mark and Matt were sitting together, the boy on his grandfather's lap. They were teasing and laughing with each other as they so often did.

"Matt," Martin said in the middle of the prayer, consciously avoiding any coercion, "do you think you can do something difficult?" He was already in tears. "Are you able to look beyond this happy scene to the one we're both sensing is to follow? We can tell that you and Mark are aware of a bright light in front of you. You know that the light is Jesus and you both want to greet him. And, Matt, we see that Jesus is inviting Mark to go with him to the joyful setting that the Spirit has just taught us about, our real home, heaven. Matt, are you able to give Mark that last hug now? We see that he doesn't want you to hurt, he loves you so, but he knows that he has to go with Jesus."

Matt sobbed. "This is hard, this is very hard." The words faltered as he was overcome by tears. But in a few seconds it was done. He had given his grandson to God, knowing all the while that it was only a temporary parting. The painful knot in his chest disappeared. The weight lifted. The tears stopped suddenly.

Matt composed himself, then looked at Martin. "I'm alright. That was hard. I've never done anything harder in my life. But I'm okay now."

And Matt really was okay. When he arrived for his return visit two weeks later, the depression had lifted; Matt was a new man! His activities and relationships had taken on a new meaning because he had experienced the healing touch of Jesus. Matt's newfound experience of God had completely changed the way he thought about life. That transformation had resulted in profound changes that affected the way he related to others, particularly those in his family. Through a phone call some months later, we were glad to hear that Matt has maintained his healing by walking in the truth and freedom of Christ.

How very much God wants each of us to be whole. Even Matt—who had lived what he thought to be sixty-four perfect years—discovered that he needed to make some significant adjustments to experience true, lasting freedom. It was more than simply grief over his loss. He had a deep, aching need to grow spiritually.

But he wouldn't surrender his life to God's healing touch until he was forced to during a time of profound helplessness. In his vulnerability, he experienced the love of God breaking through into his life in a completely new way. In fact, after experiencing healing in his life, Matt discovered a dimension of wholeness he had never even thought he needed!

What exactly do we mean by wholeness? We've mentioned it a number of times in different contexts.

Wholeness is a word which came into popular usage through the pop psychology movement of the 1960s and 1970s. During the ensuing me-decade, a large number of books and organizations have appeared espousing what is known as holistic health. Recently, a concept of wholeness has also been popularized among Christians by a growing number of books and ministries focused on inner healing. Wholeness, therefore, has both secular and Christian connotations. Unfortunately, many Christians have been misled about the true meaning of wholeness, because they have drawn upon both Christian and secular meanings of the concept without good judgment or discernment.

Our understanding of wholeness proceeds from basic Christian truth: God loves each human being, for he has created each of us in his own image and likeness. He wants each of us to experience that love forever with him in heaven. Wholeness is the security that comes from realizing this truth fully in every circumstance of life. When we have that security, we can live in the freedom, dignity, and personal strength that God intends for us as his sons and daughters. Then we can bear fruit for God in our daily lives, particularly in our relationships with others.

When one knows at the core of his being that he is loved by God, the deep craving for human affirmation subsides. Whether one is loved or unloved by the world, the assurance of divine love is enough to prevent undue reliance on approval and acceptance by others. Human beings are very vulnerable to the pain of indifference, rejection, and psychological and emotional attack without this kind of assurance.

Matt's healing exemplifies this understanding of true wholeness for us. He had a deep yearning for a son that he could love and who would love him in return. His grandson filled that deep human need in Matt. Therefore, when his grandson was suddenly taken from him, he experienced a profound sense of loss. Matt could only receive wholeness after he let his grandson go and let the healing love of God flood his soul, bringing restoration and new meaning to his life.

For Matt and for all of us, the reality of true wholeness is good news. The eternal happiness that Christianity promises begins on earth, because God desires good things for us in this world. "I came," Jesus says, "that they might have life and have it to the full" (Jn 10:10). But eternal happiness is not limited to the realities of this life. We need to keep this in mind as well. Yet this is the deceptive and dangerous view held out to us by holistic medicine and many other secular philosophies of life.

We need to remember that the road to eternal life sometimes means accepting pain, failure, and other kinds of suffering that most secular philosophies are unwilling to have us accept. After all, Jesus himself—he who embraced the cross for our sake—tells us that "narrow is the gate that leads to life, how rough the road, and how few there are who find it!" (Mt 7:14).

In our wounded world today, there are many people who have found a measure of wholeness. Some of them have endured excruciating deprivation, emotional and physical assault, and even untold misery. In the midst of all the pain they have come to grasp the central sustaining truth that God loves them. They can stand secure in their identity as sons and daughters of God. This saving knowledge equips them for fruitful lives in the kingdom of God.

Tragically, there are others whose pain so dominates their lives that it consumes all of their energy, eroding their capacity to rest in the knowledge of God's sustaining love. These are the walking wounded of the world who desperately need the grace of inner healing.

One stormy afternoon Gloria came to us. Her painful past had left her embittered and crippled emotionally and spiritually. Could God break through and deliver her? Could he heal her failed marriage? Could the Lord save a woman who was filled with so much self-hatred and hatred of men in general?

FIVE

The Many Glorias in Our World

G LORIA HATED MEN. She hated them with a passion. After several pastoral counseling sessions at her church had proven fruitless, she came to us with her problem.

She complained to us about her failing marriage. But we quickly discovered Gloria's marriage was only the staging ground for acting out a deep self-loathing as well as a deep-seated hatred of all men. Gloria had been told that God loved her and that only by turning to Christ could she find effective help. Yet her bitter experiences as a child growing up in an abusive home had left Gloria unable to relate to God as a loving Father.

It wasn't hard to see why. Gloria identified all men with her brutal, alcoholic father who had abused her emotionally, physically, and sexually from childhood almost up to the very day she married. The only other significant male in her life was her brother Albert. And during their teenage years, Albert copied the behavior of his father, abusing his poor sister in almost every way imaginable.

The years of mental torture and physical abuse by the most important men in Gloria's life took an enormous toll emotionally and psychologically. She survived only by repressing her growing feelings of hatred and worth-lessness, refusing to confront the severity of her problem. Like many women in an abusive situation, she only wanted a way out. Marriage became her avenue of escape.

Her marriage to Randy was as much an escape from her abusive family as it was a flight into the arms of her Prince Charming. The reason for Randy's charm was straight-forward. A gentle and patient man, he was a welcome contrast to Gloria's own father.

But the charm wore off quickly. Randy had a facial anomaly. This defect began to obsess Gloria, and she could think of nothing else. The seething rage that had built up over the years against her father and brother finally surfaced. But she didn't vent it against the perpetrators. Instead, she turned on her innocent and bewildered husband. Even the lunches she reluctantly packed for him served as an outlet for this deep-seated anger. For instance, she would crush his potato chips or spoil his food in other ways out of spite.

Her rage and hatred began to destroy her marriage. But Gloria was destroying herself most of all. She became a shattered and crippled human being.

Then one day this sad woman—who refused to con-front the reasons why she hated her husband, resented her two children, and despised herself—cried out in des-peration to God. In that moment of desperate prayer, she encountered Jesus as her merciful savior. She knew that Jesus had heard her anguished cry and would provide a way out of her misery. But the way out proved to be a series of confrontations with divine love that were almost too much for Gloria to handle.

She found it very difficult to accept her infinite worth as a daughter of God in the eyes of her loving heavenly

Father, because the only father she had ever known had given her a very different view of herself. And how could she yield to the compelling invitation of Jesus to trust in his redeeming love for her? The only brotherly relationship she had ever known was a mockery of brotherly love. And to top it all off, how could she embrace the gift of life when her sister had chosen death? Right at the start of our counseling relationship with Gloria, her sister— plagued by similar problems—committed suicide at the very hospital where she had just been admitted for her own protection! Clearly, if anyone had a good reason to give up and wallow in hatred, despair, and self-pity—that person was Gloria.

Yet miraculously Gloria did accept God's love. She chose to yield to God's healing and saving grace. And good things began to happen.

When we started counseling her, the sessions were electric with conflict. Gloria wanted to lash out at Martin because she loathed his maleness. But she kept returning and began opening herself up to the power of healing through the use of imagery inspired by the Holy Spirit. We would begin and conclude each session with prayer for the specific grace Gloria needed to yield to God's love and respond to him. Gradually, she was able to face the abuse that had been meted out to her and forgive both her father and brother. She finally began to experience God's love for her and repented for her warped view of Randy.

Within a few months Gloria was a new person! God had worked a miracle in her heart. Her anger had subsided, and her dormant love for Randy had been stirred up in her heart. She now saw her children as great cause for joy rather than as objects of her displaced aggression. The healing love of God the Father and Jesus had replaced every defective stereotype that had poisoned Gloria's concept of men. Even Randy experienced healing. He had suffered from chronic impotence, and this condition was cured after only three counseling sessions.

Randy and Gloria then experienced the release of the power and the joy of the Holy Spirit in their lives. In fact, after only a few months of counseling, the emotional chaos left by years of unspeakable trauma had been largely removed; and they were behaving like newlyweds. They were well on their way to living lives rooted in prayer and supported by a caring Christian community. Gloria called to tell us six months after her counseling ended that she and Randy were still "like new persons."

In Gloria's case Christian counseling was empowered by an inner healing ministry. Through this dynamic combination, she and many other people have been helped to "put on a new self which will progress toward true knowledge the more it is renewed in the image of its Creator" (Col 3:10). Gloria would certainly not have experienced the kind of wholeness God wanted for her without this kind of intervention. Inner healing allowed Gloria to see her brokenness for what it really was: the unacceptable outcome of the sins of others against God's beloved child; and her equally unacceptable responses in lashing out at others, particularly her innocent husband.

Our experience with Gloria shows how effective pastoral counseling and inner healing can be. Tragically, there are many Glorias in our world: people who are unable to come into the wholeness held out to all who taste of the freedom of God's love.

Inner healing is for them. The details may differ from individual to individual. The process itself varies in each case. But the need is always much the same. Inner healing is necessary to the degree that one's brokenness and pain prevent him from experiencing God's perfect love.

In a real sense, this is an obligatory grace. God's mercy requires that it be offered and our need obliges us to seek it. We need to get away from the false idea that it's an extra—an option we can accept or reject at our own whim. Creator and creature have a destiny: a communion of love that is meant to be eternal. And in a cooperative venture involving the truth in love through the grace of inner healing, the fragments of a shattered personality come together. God restores what is lacking. He empowers and equips us. And the creative communion that he desires with his child can proceed. As a first priority, then, the follower of Jesus will want to face squarely whatever it is that deters him from thoroughly appropriating God's love. A Christian can tell how thoroughly God's love is being appropriated when he becomes less and less dependent on the affirmation of others and capricious circumstances for his sense of well-being. God's mercy has then reached its target. His love and truth—which are always ministered together in the realm of the Spirit—have been apprehended by the soul. From there God's truth and love begin to permeate the whole person, bringing the healing and restoration that was never thought possible.

That deep sense of well-being that comes from a thorough appreciation of God's personal love is just another way of describing wholeness. And both of these terms describe that remarkable state of complete contentment or interior satisfaction that the Hebrew language sums up in the word "shalom." Much more than simply peace—which is often used as a synonym for shalom—it means utter peacefulness.

When a believer is completely aware of how God's personal love is nurturing every cell in his body with perfect wisdom and knowledge, no wind of circumstance or idle whim of another can ruffle his abiding sense of shalom in God. That, our brothers and sisters, is true wholeness. That is the first priority of inner healing and pastoral counseling for Christians.

Secular psychology wants us to believe that wholeness is self-discovery. But, as we have seen, true wholeness is much more than that. It is a radically new form of self-awareness. It is the awareness that my self, to the fullest sense possible, is loved by my heavenly Father.

This liberating knowledge carries with it the inner prompting to make an appropriate response to God. Knowing I am so fully loved by God frees me from craving the love of others. It frees me from undue self-concern. It frees me to love Jesus more completely, even when it hurts. I begin to see that it is only through his sacrifice on the cross that I am able to stand in the Father's presence as a child of God.

This blessed freedom unlocks a deep yearning to love God the Father in a new way—as wholly as I am now whole—and to love my neighbor as much as my newly discovered, lovable self.

God intends this kind of love for everyone, not just a select few. And many people do achieve some measure of wholeness in the ordinary flow of the Christian life. But many do not. It is precisely for these people that the ministry of inner healing can prove most effective.

A few years ago a woman named Anna came to see us. Anna's problem didn't spring from an abusive family situation. She came from a very good home and a loving family. The emotional trauma that had crippled her was much more subtle than most of the cases we have presented so far.

However, the experience we had counseling and praying with Anna can help all of us understand how even subtle emotional trauma can trouble a person so deeply that one's self-image and relationships with others are seriously damaged.

In fact, in Anna's case, inner healing literally made the difference between life and death.

SIX

The Eternal Perspective

A TALENTED MUSICIAN, ANNA had to take a leave of absence from the conservatory where she was studying because of stress. When she arrived for her first appointment with Martin, she was unduly distraught. She had secrets to reveal and wondered if it was safe to entrust them to a stranger. But as she opened her heart to us, she began to discover the one who could truly help her: the Lord Jesus.

Anna's biggest secret was that she "made herself get sick" whenever the stress became too great for her to handle. For many weeks this had been a constant occurrence. She was a victim of an eating disorder called bulimia. Anna went on eating binges which were followed by violent vomiting purges. She thought she was doing this to control her weight, but the truth about this frail young woman was that her bulimia proved to be just another symptom of her perfectionism which was rooted in an underlying sense of worthlessness. She always had to prove herself.

Since early childhood Anna had won numerous academic and musical honors, but it was never enough. She hoped against hope that one day she would jump through the right hoop, one high enough and flaming enough to give her relief from a constant effort to satisfy the critics in her family and her academic circle.

But not one of the gold medals did the trick.

It was quickly apparent that Anna's struggle for self-acceptance was rooted in something even more fundamental than parental attitudes or behavior. These indeed played a part, but what Anna was really searching for was the fundamental meaning of existence itself. And this search was leading her to God.

Anna was Jewish, but her fast-paced lifestyle in an affluent West Coast community left little time for her or her socially active family to pay much attention to the spiritual treasures of their ancestral heritage. Finally, in the context of intolerable unhappiness and a deep sense of meaninglessness, Anna was beginning to sort through this treasury. What she eventually found was much more than her Jewish identity as a member of the chosen people. She found the very one who chose her and her people in the first place.

"What can I do about this?" Anna pleaded as we showed her the way to fulfill her longing to know the Messiah. "My family will kill me. I'll be worse off than ever."

But she was better off than ever. She began to read the Bible and some books that helped answer the important questions that were surfacing during our counseling sessions. She discovered that the works of C.S. Lewis were especially well suited for her intellectual inquiry into the faith. She also began to see her emotions in their proper role as servants in her struggle to learn self-acceptance and to accept God's love.

Anna finally decided to give the dynamic reality of prayer a try. Prayer during counseling sessions and outside of them eventually helped her make the decision that was to change her life forever.

We ended each counseling session by praying in the name of Jesus the Messiah, remembering Anna's blood-line. United with Jesus through the common ancestor of Abraham, Anna took this prayer to heart and began to pray to Jesus each day. As she turned to the Messiah, he fulfilled his mission in her life. "The spirit of the Lord is upon me; therefore he has anointed me. He has sent me to bring glad tidings to the poor, to proclaim liberty to captives, recovery of sight to the blind and release of prisoners, to announce a year of favor from the Lord" (Lk 4:18-19). This became Anna's herald call as she responded to Jesus the Savior.

Her leave of absence, a real sabbatical, truly became a year of favor from the Lord. Anna was able to live off campus in a house with several Christian women rather than in the mandatory dormitory setting. Her Messiah proclaimed the good news of unconditional acceptance in his sight. And he did restore her sight spiritually, so that Anna could see her family and her academic peer relationships through his eyes. He released her from captivity to bulimia by showing her that he was in control. He showed Anna that he would provide her with incorruptible manna to fill her needs for daily sustenance, even as he provided for her ancestors during their sojourn in the desert.

One evening while praying in her own quiet room, Anna met the Messiah in a profound and personal way. There in the presence of all the truth that she was able to handle about her own identity, he revealed himself to her in a way she could understand. During a moment of sovereign grace, he filled Anna with his Holy Spirit and a new song burst forth from her lips. A new language of praise flowed from her like rivers of living water sounding the depths within. Anna had been completely reborn. Spiritually and emotionally she was not the same woman who had walked into our office a few months earlier.

Anna returned to school and began helping other music students cope with the special stress that we have come to call "conservatory syndrome." She understood deeply the truths and deceptions connected with self-esteem and self-absorption. Anna witnessed to struggling students about her own battle with perfectionism and the wonderful freedom she had found in abandoning all to the providence of Jesus the Messiah.

Anna also witnessed about Jesus to members of her family. Through this she began to learn what it means to be strong in the truth, while loving those who cannot yet accept the truth. She began to see what it means to suffer persecution for the love of God. Over time she learned that following the Messiah through the waters of baptism sometimes means following him through the fires of baptism. Because of the credible witness of a transformed Anna, an older sister—also a musician—accepted Jesus as her Lord.

Anna is now walking in a new dimension of wholeness. She knows with every fiber of her being that the heavenly Father loves her so much that he sent her people the Messiah to endure the cross. She knows that he loves her so much that he permits her to follow in his footsteps along the path to holiness. Anna is now giving her life as a love offering to him.

And in the unending exchange of love that authentic healing releases, the Lord adds grace upon grace. He has led Anna triumphant through the rigors of the conservatory, through the juries, the auditions, into a professional world of performance and teaching where her fulfilled Judaism wins many souls to his kingdom. He has led Anna into the arms of a wonderful young minister to whom she is now engaged and in whose congregation her musical gift extols the mercy of God for all to hear and see. Love begetting love in an endless circle that has no room for self-doubt, self-punishment, or self-absorption. That has spelled wholeness for Anna.

A common thread in inner healing for each of the people you have met in this book—Martin, Sally, Matt, Gloria, and Anna—is that wholeness was achieved in the context of a profound conversion experience. In every case there was an explicit acceptance of Jesus Christ as personal Lord and savior. There was heartfelt repentance for one's own sins. There was a commitment to ongoing conversion through authentic Christian living.

We have also pointed out that healing is not for this life only. Rather, it is for this life and the next. In fact, one of the basic beliefs of Christianity is that earthly life is only a pilgrimage toward that eternal happiness which is our ultimate goal. Heaven is our true home. In this light, we see that achieving greater wholeness in this life is only eternally important when it serves to prepare us for the next life. Wholeness really should lead to holiness, to a desire for holiness, to a commitment to appropriate God's grace which moves us towards holiness.

If this is not occurring as we pray with people and counsel them, then we are falling short in our Christian duty. If we do not encourage the men and women we counsel to want to follow Jesus with all their mind, heart, soul, and strength—then our work is essentially no different from that of secular therapists whose sole concern is for the temporal welfare of their clients rather than their eternal welfare.

If we are to operate in an explicitly Christian ministry, we must be prepared to teach the brothers and sisters we help the overriding importance of an eternal perspective on life. Most people today live their lives with only an earthly perspective in view. They live for today and plan only for their earthly future. They plan for retirement income and their children's education. Few people, it seems, judge their daily lives on the basis of what kind of an afterlife their behavior is preparing them for. An eternal perspective equips us to live daily life with the knowledge and conviction that our eternal destiny is to be with God in heaven. That means our behavior in this life results either in eternal life with God in heaven, or eternal separation from him.

However, an eternal perspective means more than the certainty of eternal life in either heaven or hell. It also means that Christians begin to move away from looking at situations with the limited eyes of the flesh and begin to see things the way God sees them. The best explanation we have seen of this comes from Ralph C. Martin, a Christian evangelist and teacher whom we admire. Here's how he describes the eternal perspective:

Scripture says that "every thought must be made captive to Christ." This means that the way we think about things needs to be changed to conform with the way things are. The way we know how things are is by conforming ourselves to the mind of Christ. Here is how St. Paul puts it:

"There is, to be sure, a certain wisdom which we express among the spiritually mature. It is not a wisdom of this age, however, nor of the rulers of this age, who are men headed for destruction. No, what we utter is God's wisdom, a mysterious, hidden wisdom.

... Of this wisdom it is written: Eye has not seen, ear has not heard, nor has it so much as dawned on man what God has prepared for those who love him. Yet, God has revealed this wisdom to us, through the Spirit." (1 Cor 2:6-10)

Some of us, when we first read this passage, read the verse, "eye has not seen, ear has not heard... what God has prepared for those who love him" as the promise of something that is coming when we get to heaven. Certainly, the full measure of it is coming in heaven. But the passage goes on to say that God has revealed this wisdom to us here and now on earth.

Christians have been given the ability to see, hear, and understand things beyond mere human understanding through the Holy Spirit. Only people living in union with Christ and who have formed their lives according to his word can possibly understand what is going on in the world today. We are the only ones in a position to understand, because only God sees and knows what is going on, and he makes these things known to us through his word and his Spirit.

Our Christian faith is a revelation of the structure of reality. It is not an optional spiritual hobby. It is not only something that enriches our lives or helps us be more devotional. Christianity is a revelation of the structure of the universe. It puts us in touch with the most important things in the universe, things we could not perceive solely through the human senses. (*FireWatch* Newsletter; February 1986, p. 7.)

Here is the mind of God laid bare before us—his overriding eternal perspective which gives ultimate meaning and purpose to our lives.

Anna's healing is illuminated by this heavenly perspective. We see that the decisive point for her healing was conversion to Jesus Christ as the Messiah. Once she had taken on that perspective, she was able to appropriate the healing and saving grace she so desperately needed. Thus, Anna was able to choose life and reject death in the fullest sense possible as a new creation in Christ. And, of course, she could not help but proclaim that new life to her family and her academic circle of friends.

Alice, another one of our clients, had to learn to see herself through the eyes of the Lord, taking on his perspective. Alice came to us seeking help for her thirteen-year-old daughter Maggie.

Maggie's problems were not academic ones. She had difficulties adjusting socially. Maggie was particularly bothered by Carla, a classmate with a very dominant personality who was unduly influencing her. Maggie even feigned sickness at times to avoid Carla's pesky dominance.

After a few counseling sessions with Maggie and Alice, it became clear that the girl's social maladjustment and personal insecurity was but a pale reflection of her mother's far more significant problems. It turns out Alice had been saddled with the emotional and psychological pain of a devastating physical injury that she had sustained nearly forty years earlier.

At first, Alice wanted us to focus on the cluster of behaviors that were associated with her painfully shy manner in social situations. She wanted to stop being so self-conscious about the leg injury which had left her disabled. But her anger at the inept medical treatment she had suffered and anger at her mother and aunt for their insensitivity to her prolonged hospitalization—all this needed to be dealt with first.

Alice's problems were compounded by a ruthless guilt that obsessed her. "Why did I run out into the street when my aunt warned me to watch where I was going? Why didn't I tell the nurses, the doctors, and my relatives how much pain I was experiencing in my leg? Why didn't I insist that my mother do something about the cruel treatment I was receiving at the hospital during those endless days and nights? Those endless days and nights when the misaligned bones and the stubborn infection were under the care of someone who was too busy to realize that I wasn't just another whining brat looking for attention? And why haven't I had stronger faith during recent years to receive the physical healing I believe that God is more than able to grant me even now?"

Deep-seated frustration, guilt, and bitterness were all buried in the heart of this meek, reserved woman. Yet underneath this burden of pain and misery, we discovered an extraordinarily sensitive person, a woman who had uncanny insight into the hearts of others, a woman of unflagging faith.

We explored different facets of her psychological trauma during each of our counseling sessions. As is our custom, we began and ended all of the sessions with prayer. We also followed the promptings of the Holy Spirit as he gave us spiritual insight into each area of concern.

Eventually, Alice moved from the stance of an angry, guilt-ridden seeker of physical healing to the stance of a child of God who had been freed from self-contempt. She no longer needed to be ashamed of the visible stigma of her bitter accident. All of this was able to happen as Alice—who had been a fatherless child—experienced the loving care of God the Father for the first time in her life.

On the day of her breakthrough, Alice was in a state of elation and turned on her car radio to find some joyful tune to match her mood. The song the station played just as she turned on the radio was the golden oldie, "Daddy's Little Girl." God the Father wanted Alice to remember the truth of his unconditional love for her as a daughter. Her natural ears and her heart needed to perceive that truth from the perspective of God as the loving Father.

Emotional healing led Alice into new depths of spiritual growth as she saw life through the eyes of the heavenly Father. She was able to forgive the doctors, her mother, and her aunt for the agony which followed her tragic accident. By accepting her deformity and learning to live with it, she began to see others who were suffering with the compassion of Christ. God began to use her gift of extraordinary sensitivity in ministering to others.

Yes, God wants to heal us so that we can be whole. But more to the point, he wants us to take on his mind and heart. He wants us to see things the way they really are. Then we can begin to experience wholeness and holiness as a way of life in Christ. As Mother Teresa of Calcutta put it, "It is nothing extraordinary to be holy."

However, most people caught in the midst of unbearable suffering look for the "quick fix." This is a mistake because—even though emotional suffering is an evil God did not originally intend for us—it can be a source of life-changing grace for those who turn to God. It is truly tragic when getting relief from pain becomes more important than coming into a life-changing relationship with the holy and eternal God.

The quest for wholeness can then block God's call to know and love him. "I want to be whole" quickly becomes translated into "get rid of my suffering." Although it is understandable from a human perspective, such a pursuit of relief can sabotage the ultimate redemptive value of suffering.

A young man freed from drug addiction, Rick discovered the hard way that a "quick fix" is not God's "best fix." How could Rick find real peace and fulfillment?

SEVEN

Seeking the Gift but Not the Giver

R ICK CAME TO A HEALING SERVICE out of desperation. He wanted relief from his deep-seated emotional pain and had decided that his former solution—escaping into the counterculture of drugs—had only compounded his suffering. The power of God fell mightily on those gathered in the auditorium. The anointed praise of God's people paved the way for the featured speaker and her message. It was the kind of message Rick desperately wanted to hear: "God loves you, and wants to set you free tonight."

And it happened. Rick was freed from the physiological and psychological compulsions that had prompted him to seek drugs as an avenue of escape and relief. But that is all that happened. And Rick needed much more than simply immediate relief from his addiction to drugs. This young man was suffering from the devastating consequences of a very unstable early childhood, which included a self-destructive lifestyle that centered on drug abuse.

That night Rick thought he had found what he needed. But he didn't find lasting peace and fulfillment until years later. Then in even deeper desperation, he cried out to God, "I need you, Lord."

Rick told us in counseling about his delayed response to that earlier moment of grace at the healing service. Now he is a vibrant, young Christian leader who has been blessed with both natural charisma and spiritual gifts. Yet he laments the years he lost because of delaying his conversion—because of seeking only the gift and not the giver. He now sees those precious years as time wasted, his mortal life and immortal soul needlessly jeopardized. He had squandered the grace of his healing because he had been attracted to the wrong thing: only the promise of relief and not the challenge of a life-sustaining personal relationship with the Most High. Rick vowed that he would never extend the gift of healing to someone without being sure that authentic evangelization was the primary motive. God's *real* mercy is the revelation of his holiness, his call to follow in Jesus' footsteps by living a holy life. Rick now understood that profound truth of God's kingdom.

But, in counseling, it became clear that the fault was not only Rick's. He had not been presented with the challenge of conversion at the anointed prayer service where he had been healed. He didn't recognize his need for conversion. Rick only saw his all-consuming need for release from a painful addiction. In a sense, it was less Rick's fault than the fault of the empowered minister of healing who had isolated the element of healing from the integrated work of healing and conversion.

Tragically, Rick is only one of many sufferers who have shared with us their stories of protracted distress, which were caused because either they or ministers of healing missed the important point of conversion. In our prayer ministry, we listen carefully for what we call the spiritual affect that accompanies the content of a client's story. Sometimes we find ourselves getting restless and concerned as the narrative runs on and on. We begin to suspect that our client is missing the point of inner healing: conversion to God.

"What isn't connecting here?" we ask ourselves, taking mental notes. "All the words seem to be right. This person has brought his experience to us for prayer. He says that he is open to the Lord. He wants to understand his painful experiences from God's perspective. So what's wrong?"

Invariably, it is the spiritual *affect* of the sharing that makes us uneasy and tips us off that something is wrong. The words do not match the emotions or feelings expressed in the narrative. We aren't just talking about the obvious personal and interpersonal feelings that are part of the dynamics of counseling. No, we're also talking about the tone, the mood—the spiritual testimony of the person's inner life which he projects in counseling. This is the interior life where God and man commune. And this is what we find is out of sync.

We listen and wait for an opportunity to serve as a collective memory for the person—the way the storytellers in biblical days recounted the heroic deeds of God's anointed and reminded the people of God's action in their midst in times of need. We wait for the moment when we can say, "Do you remember when you experienced the burden lifting? Do you remember when we prayed together and you came into the holy presence of God the Father? Remember how the things that seemed to be bothering you so much seemed to disappear as you meditated on God's love for you and his truth? Remember?"

What we find is that when the spiritual affect is off-base in counseling, the focus on private prayer and reflection in the individual's life at home has also been off-center. It is important to encourage such people in distress to really seek the Lord and his presence in daily prayer and throughout their day as well. They need to see that the real agenda has been, "Lord, heal my distress." They need to reach the point where they can honestly say, "Lord, simply come and be with me in my distress. I want you."

We are so utterly convinced of God's desire to make himself known to everyone that we have confidence he will accomplish this kind of a turnaround when he brings people to us who are in distress. We need to listen carefully for the real message behind what is being shared. We need to discern through the Holy Spirit the spiritual *affect* of the one who trusts us enough to share his problems. The true agenda is then rarely hidden. Is it, "Take away my pain, Lord?" Or is it, "Show yourself to me, O Lord?"

Our goal is to guide the sufferer to the Lord himself. There, lasting consolation finds its home. When the goal of "relief" is stubbornly clung to, disappointment and frustration inevitably result. The burning desire God has to make himself known is blocked by our own selfishness and self-concern. Rick is an excellent example of this tendency. He faced greater frustration and disappointment years after his healing. He didn't experience real liberation until he freely gave his life to Jesus, the real healer.

With respect to the place of suffering in a person's life,

we are sometimes asked why the Lord seems to allow this healing process to take so long. This is occasionally asked by persons who have themselves experienced remarkable recoveries from extraordinary difficulties.

Ellen was such a person. After learning that she had been an unwanted child from the moment of conception, Ellen went into a period of inconsolable sadness, relieved only by brief outbursts of anger. This poor woman felt as if her heart had been literally broken in two.

Amazingly, Ellen's prayer life survived the grief, and she found herself talking to the Lord more frequently. For seven trying months, her only consolation was a growing intimacy with the Lord.

Then Ellen woke up one morning filled with a profound inner peace she had never tasted of before. Her broken life—her shattered self-concept—had been wondrously reassembled and made whole. All of a sudden Ellen was able to tolerate her parents' weaknesses and deficiencies, particularly their inability to show her the love she had so desperately needed as a child. The Lord had mended Ellen's broken heart in his own time and in his own way.

Most important of all, Ellen knew God had answered her plaintive cry during those long and sorrowful months. "Why, Lord, are you taking so long to bring me out of this pain?" Ellen had cried out. And God the Father had etched the answer on her heart in the language of divine love: "I am your Father, and you are my daughter. I will never leave you or forsake you."

Ellen now realized that those difficult seven months had been just long enough for her to learn the important spiritual lesson that a quicker healing would not have conveyed: the unshakable realization that her heavenly

Father would be ever-present to her in the midst of joys and sorrows, everywhere and always! What a blessing in disguise that trying time actually proved to be.

Ellen's protracted time of sorrow had opened up the window of opportunity for a deep awakening of faith in her. She now accepted without doubt that God is indeed our Emmanuel, "God-with-us." He doesn't desert his children and leave them orphaned. Ellen experienced a newfound relationship with God the Father. She could now say with her whole heart: "God is with me."

From Ellen's experience and those of many Ellens in our ministry, we have come to appreciate the value of the trying times of extended unanswered prayer. We see the value of waiting on the Lord. Our task, as facilitators in healing, is to offer encouragement and hope—sometimes by simply being there. Our task is not to contrive an easy solution and back away from the need to persevere in seeking God's mind. Nor is it our job to offer excuses for God. It isn't as if he needs someone to cover up for his dereliction of duty in not sparing us from sorrow. We need to remember that God sees the whole picture. He knows what we can handle. He knows when and how to answer our prayers.

For a good number of us, to be spared sorrow might well mean to be spared the most gracious of all graces: an enduring, unshakable personal relationship with God. It may well take seven months or even longer for sorrow to produce the full supply of heavenly nectar our souls so desperately need to draw near to God. In fact, we believe this is one aspect of the refreshing "living water" of the gospel that is meant to characterize the inner life of the Christian. Jesus wants to be an unfailing source of consolation for each of us.

By keeping this principle in mind, we have learned an important lesson in compassionate companionship. It is the lesson of merciful restraint, an expression of the confidence we have that God will commune with those who cry out to him in their distress. It is the lesson of letting go, even while being present at healing sessions. We call it "staying with."

If we can manage this delicate intervention—that is, staying with those who are suffering as opposed to hanging on to them—we can provide a consistent witness of God's truth and love that allows the sufferer to enter the furnace of affliction with understanding. Then that affliction can yield its pure gold in Christ as it is tested and refined by fire.

Relying on His Servants But Not on the Lord Himself

Yet we have learned not only to stay with people but to "stay back" at the Lord's leading. This interpersonal healing principle is based on the same sure conviction that a lifelong, life-changing relationship with the Lord is God's desire for the afflicted one who is so often consumed with the content of his distress. Just as the gift of healing can prove an obstacle to this relationship, so can God's servants and instruments.

We have learned from some of our distressed clients that too much availability, too many counseling sessions, and too much healing prayer can foster a subtle, skewed focus. Instead of growing in his attachment to God, we find the client moving toward an attachment to the Lord's servants.

Deborah's healing demonstrated that we could trust a certain inner guidance to stay back and position ourselves in the background, while always remaining very much concerned. We began to see the power of a paradox in our ministry. We need to set limits on our accessibility, yet we want to stay connected. We do not want to encourage increased contact, yet we want to remain available. We want to foster solitude with the Lord, while also mitigating the damaging effects of loneliness and feelings of rejection.

Even in the midst of another's great travail, we could reduce the frequency and intensity of our personal interventions dramatically. We have learned to use the growth-producing gift of staying back by verbalizing our confident reliance on the sufferer's ability to see it through with God one on one. By that we mean without someone else's special prayers or words of counsel.

It has become clear that the Lord wants us to be as small as possible in the eyes of those we are privileged to help. It is God and him alone to whom we must direct the sufferer's attachments and affections. The simple and sincere assurance that we are experiencing empathy with the sufferer is often enough to set in motion the grace of bonding to the Lord.

With Deborah, her near-suicide and the intensity of her subsequent medical and psychiatric rehabilitation left little doubt that her chronic depression was nothing to treat lightly. She had had a significant conversion experience some time before her frighteningly close call with a massive drug overdose. But her response to healing ministry—as she experienced it in Bible studies and prayer groups she attended—was somehow off. After a period of counsel and prayer, we could see how much Deborah's anguish consumed her. We began to see how much it might have consumed us, too.

Deborah's situation was pathetic. Her problem took the form of a dependency neurosis stemming from her fragile health and the dynamics of depressive, detached parents, along with a family pattern of alcoholism. She needed to be taken care of, yet deep down she masked that craving by setting up relationships that assured her she was essential.

Deborah's abandonment by her husband after nearly thirty years of a childless marriage proved devastating. Her chronic ill health had also progressed to the point of medical and legal disability. This meant that not even in the marketplace could Deborah act out her deep desire to be needed, much less her need to receive at least some symbolic expressions of being cared for.

No wonder her suicide attempt had been more than just an attention-grabbing gesture. Deborah truly wanted to end a life that only held suffering and misery for her.

But what about the saving power of Jesus? Hadn't Deborah given her life to him? And the brothers and sisters of her Bible study, prayer group, and new congregation—why weren't they able to open the way to healing and abundant life for her? What about all of the counsel and healing ministry she had received? Wasn't that God's special provision for Deborah's healing and reason for hope? What was wrong?

Ultimately, it became clear to us that all the prayer, all the memorizing of Scripture, all the counseling and ministering had been sought with the best of intentions; but it had not been set in the context of meeting God in a relationship without any contingencies or conditions. Deborah, underneath it all, needed to be cared for. She had never dared to enter a relationship without somehow contriving it into a helper-helpee format.

We saw that underneath it all—beneath her deep-seated interpersonal need for love from others—was the even greater need to experience the person of Jesus and the person of God the Father without extensive "third-party" mediation. She needed God most of all and not people.

We took a calculated risk and suggested that we not use the standard inner healing approach of constructing a visualized scene where Jesus would make his appearance and remove the pain from her or take her out of the pain. Deborah seemed so fragile and had always relied on others to pray for her. We needed to take a different tack.

Well-intentioned Christian friends and popular healing ministers had reinforced her dependency and self-doubt by drawing from their repertoires predictable prayer scenarios for her. The Holy Spirit had not only been preempted by these earnest ministers of God's mercy, but Deborah herself had grown to demean her own simple language of faith. She became convinced that her own homely attempts at praying for healing were too unrefined and amateurish to be granted by the Lord.

What we were proposing was perhaps too simple: invite Jesus into your distress. You can do it. Paint no word pictures. Suggest no expectation of relief. Place no conditions, no petitions, or demands before the holy one. Only ask him to be with you in the midst of your pain.

We expected Deborah to balk at our suggestions. Imagine our surprise when she readily accepted what we had to say. As if a light bulb had suddenly been turned on, she simply said, "All right. I think I see what you mean."

The prayer we said was extremely simple: "Lord Jesus Christ, Deborah has cried out to you for help in so many ways. Now we ask you not for help but for yourself. Along with Deborah, we welcome your presence, Lord Jesus, here and now in her distress. Thank you for just being with her."

In an instant, the anointing of the Holy Spirit was upon us, and Deborah received an inner vision of Jesus. He was smiling at her, his arms folded in satisfaction and confidence. He told her, "Yes, yes, I am with you. This is what I have wanted for you all along."

Then the image of another figure, a white-haired man in a flowing green robe, flashed before Deborah. The inner knowledge that his name was Elijah came forth, and the scene developed. Elijah was on horseback, leading warriors from a triumphant battle. He extended his arms over the kneeling figure of Deborah. She heard him say, "You, too, have come to your place of triumph and rest."

Deborah had no idea why Elijah should be featured in this experience. Together we opened the Bible to First Kings, chapter nineteen. There we read about how the prophet Elijah—bereft of all hope—despairs and asks the Lord to take his life. But he is delivered from his despair through the tender mercy of the Lord Yahweh. The Lord even fortifies him with heavenly food brought by angels.

A joyful peace—resonating with the living Word of God in Scripture—now enveloped Deborah. And as the newly developed relationship with God began to grow, Deborah became a whole and holy daughter of God.

We see in Deborah's case how well-meaning therapists, counselors, or healing ministers can be obstacles to the healing God has for us. We can rely so much on their ministry and guidance that we miss the point of our healing. The point of healing is always the Lord himself and not simply the gift of healing—as was the case with Rick—or the ministry of his servants.

We can face other obstacles to the wholeness and holiness God has for us. In Steve and Nora's case, they seemed to have given their lives to the Lord. In fact, Nora had developed a growing personal relationship with the Lord. Yet their marriage and family life were fraught with conflict and tension. What was the problem?

EIGHT

Growing in Holiness

S TEVE COULD NOT UNDERSTAND why the tensions between Nora and himself had not gone away. The bickering that had characterized their stormy courtship and honeymoon had long since erupted into a predictable series of unsettled truces and bitter, physical battles. What they had to show after eleven years of a now weary marriage was the bittersweet fruit of three beautiful, painfully insecure daughters and a reservoir of resentment.

Steve and Nora had both experienced a conversion to the Lord three years earlier when Steve's mother was healed of cancer. They had learned to pray and seek God. Why hadn't that solved the problem in their marriage and in their family life?

On the recommendation of some new Christian friends, they came to us for counsel. Why, they asked us, is the tension still there? What is wrong with us?

During individual counseling sessions with each of them, we learned that both Steve and Nora had been truly touched by the grace of conversion at the time Steve's mother was healed of cancer. Nora especially had been attracted to prayer. Over time she had developed an authentic, sustaining personal relationship with the Lord.

Nora wanted to respond to the ever deepening call of conversion, and she began to change her way of reacting to Steve's provocations. As she did, the tensions between them subsided for a while. Nora looked forward to her times of personal prayer, and God honored her faithfulness to it by transforming her in different ways. Increasingly, her attitude and her behavior reflected her growing relationship with the Lord. She was loving her husband despite their marital and family problems.

Steve, on the other hand, found prayer less attractive. He is very active by nature, and his efforts to make a quiet time for God were usually characterized by dryness and distraction. His reading of Scripture proved to be particularly erratic.

Steve had a hard time with much of the Bible, classifying it as "heavy" and "judgmental." Whole passages of the Bible having to do with Christian character formation were on his handy "omit list." He would argue that the God of the Old Testament was not the same God that Jesus revealed to us in the New Testament. Steve composed an image of God that conformed to his secret attachment to another god, one his puzzled wife had never met.

When the revelation finally came, Steve was able to see the deception for what it had been all along. With a repentant heart, he told us, "I had to work hard at changing my image of God, so I wouldn't have to work hard at changing my sinful life." As attracted as he had been to the mercy of God, Steve just couldn't resist the stronger attraction to the pornography that had sullied his mind since adolescence. He seemed to recognize the conflict at first and treated the internal dissonance as a spiritual red flag, a sign that he needed to change his reading habits.

Old, bad habits, however, have a way of resisting change. Steve began to swallow the diluted gospel of God's overwhelming compassion for the human condition, along with a minimalist definition of conversion. This insidious deception put the conflict in Steve's thought life temporarily to rest.

No wonder his need for intimacy with Nora had never matured! No wonder he had failed miserably in his marital commitment to love, honor, cherish, and protect his bride. His heart had been elsewhere. No wonder there was unresolved tension in their marriage. Steve's godly inclinations had wrestled with his lustful obsessions and lost out. It came down to the fact that Steve was harboring unrepented sin and hardness of heart.

When he finally came to his spiritual senses, tears of deep repentance flowed freely. "I want only you, Lord Jesus," Steve cried out. "I don't deserve to be in your presence, but you are here. My life is all yours from now on. No more double living. No more kidding myself. Whatever it takes, I am all yours."

Steve has been true to that heartfelt confession. A new man—without self-deception and unrepented sin to insulate him from God—he now spends time each day contemplating the majesty of God. He is filling his mind with ideas that reinforce his commitment to become an image of the Lord to those around him.

Working through the consequences of years of marital distress has now become a joyful challenge for Steve and Nora. Although all of the pain hasn't gone away instantly, what was once a futile wish that things might change is now becoming a reality. Their marriage and their family is on the mend.

In Steve and Nora's case, we began to see that not only the gift and the servant but the sufferer himself can be an obstacle to God's wholeness and holiness for us. We need to truly repent of our sins from the heart. We need to put aside any unresolved hardness of heart before God can enter in with his healing power.

With Steve and Nora in mind, let's look at the bigger picture for a minute. Coming into wholeness or a practical knowledge of God's deep and abiding personal love is our short-term goal in the inner healing ministry. This goal is only the springboard to our long-term goal in ministry. Put simply, this is to lead people to the Lord, to plant in them a desire to grow in holiness. The Lord has revealed to us that when our whole being—body, mind, and spirit—longs to love God and to respond to his love for us, we are beginning our journey toward holiness.

Moving toward holiness just can't happen when we place the gift before the giver, the servant before the master, or sin and hardness of heart before seeking God alone.

This journey toward holiness is not dependent on first experiencing the Lord's healing touch in every painful memory or even every serious emotional wound we've ever experienced. Frequently, what the Lord identifies in answer to our prayer for wholeness is not the area that seems the most traumatic at the time. To the contrary, the one typically identified is the area that most blocks our reception of God's love.

Presuming or guessing is not enough in this sort of prayer. The Holy Spirit is the revealer of truth. Only reliance on his inspiration will get the job done right by identifying the correct area. When God's love and mercy finally break into our life on a deep level through this kind of prayer, our response should be a longing to be equipped for his kingdom. Our focus should not be on simply getting better equipped to cope with life's difficulties.

Unfortunately, many people find it difficult to relate to the call to be holy. The very mention of holiness sets off a series of responses that range from "I'm not ready yet" to "I want to have some fun first." Some people even conclude, "Holiness is impossible. It's just for ministers and priests, or other people like that."

Are they right? Is holiness some impossible dream? Is it some kind of sadistic plan that is impossible to achieve yet demanded by a God who wants to deprive us of every opportunity for happiness?

The answer to each of these questions is a resounding "No!" God's call to holiness reveals the intensity of his love for us. He yearns for us to draw closer to him, so that we can experience peace and joy beyond measure—so that one day we can dwell with him forever.

Look at the lives of great men and women of God like the apostle Paul, Francis of Assisi, or Mother Teresa of Calcutta in our day. They all gave up everything and suffered tremendously for the sake of holiness. Are they really so different from us? Or are they simply men and women like us who experienced God's love for them in a profound way? Was their experience of God's love so profound that they decided to spend the rest of their lives living out of love for him?

The answer is obvious, isn't it? That's the call God

issues to each one of us. It is a call to sublime happiness with God forever. It is the call to live in holiness, to grow in holiness.

The great evangelist Oswald Chambers expressed it well. He wrote in his classic work, *My Utmost for His Highest:*

"My eager desire and hope being that I may never feel ashamed, but that now as ever I may do honour to Christ in my own person by fearless courage" (Phil 1:20).

My Utmost for His Highest. "My eager desire and hope being that I may never feel ashamed." We shall all feel very much ashamed if we do not yield to Jesus on the point He has asked us to yield to Him. Paul says "My determination is to be my utmost for His Highest." To get there is a question of will, not of debate nor of reasoning, but a surrender of will, an absolute and irrevocable surrender on that point. An overweening consideration for ourselves is the thing that keeps us from that decision, though we put it that we are considering others. When we consider what it will cost others if we obey the call of Jesus, we tell God He does not know what our obedience will mean. Keep to the point; He does know. Shut out every other consideration and keep yourself before God for this one thing only—My Utmost for His Highest. I am determined to be absolutely and entirely for Him and for Him alone.

My Undeterredness for His Holiness. "Whether that means life or death, no matter!" (v. 21). Paul is determined that nothing shall deter him from doing exactly what God wants. God's order has to work up to a crisis in our lives because we will not heed the gentler way. He brings us to the place where He asks us to be our utmost for Him, and we begin to debate; then He produces a providential crisis where we have to decide—for or against, and from that point, the 'Great Divide' begins.

If the crisis has come to you on any line, surrender your will to Him absolutely and irrevocably. (Oswald Chambers, *My Utmost for His Highest;* Dodd, Mead, & Co.; New York City, 1935 and 1963; p. 1.)

Whether or not every human hurt has been healed is less important in the grand scheme of God's loving plan for us than whether or not we gain the eternal perspective on the abundant life offered to us in Christ. Being healed of the effects of insult, abandonment, abuse, loss, and disappointment is not a prerequisite for entering heaven. The Word of God tells us to "strive for holiness without which no one can see the Lord" (Heb 12:14). It also tells us, "Become holy in every aspect of your conduct" (1 Pt 1:15). Ultimately, it is holiness which equips us for our eternal destiny in Christ. All healing needs to be considered soberly with this important reality in mind.

You may be thinking, "But how can I become holy?"

Let's take Steve and Nora's story as an example and outline some simple steps. Like Steve, we need to repent of any hardness of heart or sin in our life. Then God's saving grace can break into our lives. And like Nora, we need to make a habit of seeking God every day through personal prayer and reading of Scripture. Then he can start to transform our daily lives and make us more like him. These are important first steps in leading a life of holiness.

We can also gain inspiration from the lives of holy men and women of God, such as Mother Teresa of Calcutta. We can find encouragement by reading biographies and inspirational accounts of how they have lived their lives for Christ. These are men and women who have not been strangers to pain and distress but overcomers in Christ.

In our pursuit of holiness, we can also draw upon a wealth of books written on the topic of holiness. Like Oswald Chambers, many Christian writers have written on this topic—whether from a Catholic, Protestant, or Orthodox perspective.

One of the greatest examples of inspired writing on holiness is the powerful *Prayer of St. Francis of Assisi,* a man of God revered by Protestants and Catholics alike:

Lord, make me an instrument of your peace.
Where there is hatred, let me sow love.
Where there is discord, harmony.
Where there is injury, pardon.
Where there is error, truth.
Where there is doubt, faith.
Master, grant that I may never seek
so much to be consoled as to console.
To be understood, as to understand.
To be loved, as to love with all my soul.
For it is in giving that we receive.
It is in pardoning that we are pardoned.
It is in forgetting self that we find ourselves.
And it is in dying that we are born to eternal life.

With Francis of Assisi, we see that healing which leads to holiness gets us beyond our own hurts. In fact, our experiences of pain and anguish—whether or not they are completely healed in this life—often carry with them the very graces that facilitate our sanctity.

The desire to do our "utmost for his highest," or "to love with all my soul," expresses our willingness to embrace God's plan for our lives. Grace helps us fulfill this heavenly call and gives untold meaning to our life story. The joys and sorrows of this life are not the final answer. They are transformed by Christ's redemptive suffering and the weight of glory which awaits us. With Oswald Chambers, we can echo the meditation of the apostle Paul: "My eager desire and hope being that I may never feel ashamed, but that now as ever I may do honour to Christ in my own person by fearless courage."

The real gift in earthly life is knowing that we are living fully for the Lord. Embracing the precious gift of life, with all of its marvelous opportunities for growing into the image of Christ, means being willing to embrace the unique cross he has fashioned for each of us. Being an image of the holy one and a witness for God's kingdom means being willing to identify with the crucified Savior. It means embracing the gift of life in him without conditions. It means embracing the cross for the sake of personal holiness, for the sake of growing in holiness.

But, even if we've repented of sin and fixed our eyes on Jesus, sometimes that isn't enough.

How can we ever forget that frightening night in 1974 when a pious and gentle young man came to us seeking help. A simple prayer of affirmation and renewed commitment wasn't enough. Something else needed to happen for Drew to be released from bondage.

Were we ready? Did we know what we were getting ourselves into?

NINE

Deliverance from the Evil One

W<small>E STILL REMEMBER VIVIDLY</small> that night in 1974 when Drew came to our house to receive prayer and to recommit his life to Christ. This pious and gentle young man was in the flush of his conversion back to the Catholic faith of his childhood. Drew had gone to confession earlier in the day. He had spent the whole day in prayer and fasting. Whatever influence his years as a monk in a Buddhist monastery may have had on his soul, we assumed they had been more than taken care of by his remorse-filled confession. Jesus was now undoubtedly the Lord of his life.

But to our surprise and alarm, we learned that Drew needed more than just some prayer or a renewal of commitment to be set free.

That night we joined with Drew and a couple of mature Christian friends for prayer. And something other-worldly began to manifest itself on Drew's serene, tear-stained face as we prayed. Within a minute, Drew's limbs were contorted and his facial muscles grew rigid, revealing a grotesque countenance that alarmed us all.

Drew slid to the floor and began to cry out in a strange voice that was not his own.

This was but the beginning of a battle with a legion of demons from hell whose identities had been kept deliberately hidden for years.

Ultimately, Drew was set free after an intense time spent in prayer for deliverance. We were to learn much about the evil designs of the demonic world during those two evenings of ministry. Only at the end of those two evenings could we shake hands with the *real* Drew and hug him goodbye, secure in the knowledge that he was a free man in Christ.

Why did we have to spend those two evenings praying with Drew? Exactly what is deliverance, anyway?

The New Testament tells us that Jesus not only heals the sick but also casts out evil spirits when ordinary healing and conversion of the heart aren't enough. As the Son of God and the Son of Man, he takes authority over the evil one and his demons. This important work of exorcism and deliverance is one of the signs that announces the coming of the kingdom.

In the Gospel of Luke, we learn that taking authority over the evil one is one of the first acts of Jesus upon his return from forty days of temptation in the wilderness, time spent in preparation for his public ministry. He goes to Capernaum to launch his ministry:

He then went down to Capernaum, a town of Galilee, where he began instructing them on the sabbath day. They were spellbound by his teaching, for his words had authority.

In the synagogue there was a man with an unclean spirit, who shrieked in a loud voice: "Leave us alone!

What do you want of us, Jesus of Nazareth? Have you come to destroy us? I know who you are: the Holy One of God." Jesus said to him sharply, "Be quiet! Come out of him." At that, the demon threw him to the ground before everyone's eyes and came out of him without doing him any harm. All were struck with astonishment, and they began saying to one another: "What is there about his speech? He commands the unclean spirits with authority and power, and they leave." (Lk 4:31-36)

The man who is thrown down is not simply suffering from a seizure or from an epileptic fit. The inspired Word of God tells us that a demonic presence has taken possession of the man. It takes an empowered rebuke from Jesus to cast out this evil presence.

Jesus has compassion on the afflicted man. His powerful words flow from this compassion and from his just anger toward the evil one. For Satan and his cohorts have robbed an heir of Abraham of his rightful inheritance: peace and contentment through the coming of the Messiah.

There are many other illustrations of deliverance and exorcism in the Gospels, the Acts of the Apostles, and the early history of the church. The history of Christianity is rich with documentation of this important expression of God's saving mercy, which releases his children from the kingdom of darkness by means of an empowered, authoritative unbinding in Jesus' name. In fact, in the Catholic tradition, Holy Orders—the sacrament of priesthood—imparts the Order of Exorcist during the time of priestly formation.

An important caution is in order here. We believe that

when demonic activity goes beyond harassment, obsession, or compulsion in overriding the will of the sufferer—then exorcism as a formal rite may well be in order for Roman Catholics. This might apply for example in the case of someone who has made a blood pact with the devil. This calls for more than just deliverance. Only someone with valid Orders as a priest or proper spiritual authority in another Christian tradition should undertake such a ministry.

We need to exercise caution in using deliverance. But perhaps an even greater danger is the ignorance or outright denial of supernatural evil in our modern-day culture. This simply wasn't the case generations ago when many people had a much keener awareness of the work of Satan and demons.

Martin's Great-Grandmother Knew Satan Was Real

When I was growing up, I enjoyed story times with my great-grandmother who lived with us in our household that included four generations of family members. Grandma Mayer's gift as a storyteller drew upon the richness of her long life which began in Germany and included a treasury of humorous and anecdotal tales. It was Grandma Mayer who first taught me, her "little liebchen," about the reality of spiritual warfare.

Grandma would sit in her rocking chair and tell us tales of demonic battle set deep in the heart of the Black Forest in Germany. Beyond the realm of a mere folktale or a myth, I knew that her accounts of these evil forces revealed the existence of something powerful beyond simply human or physical nature. Grandma's stories were always filled with faith. They illustrated the power of the name of Jesus and the powerful presence of Christ in the Eucharist in dispelling the evil one and his demons. These stories, which always ended on a note of victory, helped me develop an awe and respect for the cosmic conflict between good and evil.

"Never underestimate the power of the devil," Grandma used to say when obstacles to doing good showed unusual resistance to ordinary effort. "And never underestimate the power of prayer," was her inevitable corollary.

What We Have Learned about Deliverance

Today many in our skeptical society would scoff at Grandma Mayer's tales as mere superstitions. But we knew differently after praying over Drew for deliverance. We had a renewed respect and appreciation for Grandma's understanding of the spiritual reality of evil.

During those two hair-raising nights of prayer for Drew, we were shown dramatically that the *will* and the *mind* of the oppressed one is held captive by evil spirits. How clear it was that Drew wanted no part of the cunning and defiance that crossed his parched lips. Indeed, the flood of philosophizing and spiritual arrogance we heard—sometimes spoken in an oriental language unknown to Drew—was altogether unlike the contrite young man who had come to us. The will and the mind of this poor young man were not completely his own anymore. It was there that the rebuking and the reclaiming needed to be done.

We also learned that we didn't have to put up with the shenanigans and special effects that Drew's demonic oppressors were stalling us with. The haughty refusals to leave, the facial contortions, the foreign languages, and the uneasy quiet—the "eye of the hurricane"—were all quickly dismissed once we understood we had the authority of Jesus. A simple declaration was enough to force a spirit to depart: "You will *not* put on this show. You will obey and depart quietly in the holy name of Jesus Christ."

If we had learned that lesson of our authority in Jesus' name a little sooner, we could have spared Drew some pain. We could have spared him the physical pain of retching on an empty stomach and the embarrassment of hearing the sanctimonious bragging of a particular fallen angel, a spirit of false religiosity and piety who took credit for making Drew enter into a strict fast on our first day of ministry.

The Lord also taught us about the importance of the charismatic gifts of the Spirit in deliverance, particularly discernment of spirits. At first we were uncertain what we should do with thoughts of this or that, with a name or a description that came to mind, as we prayed. But Sally soon realized that these were the personal identities of evil spirits that were preying upon Drew's will, his character, and his personality.

When these evil spirits were forced to acknowledge their identity, we discovered that we had the authority to call them by name and cast them out with Jesus' authority. Over time we've grown to expect that the Holy Spirit will supply us with this important gift whenever we have need for deliverance in inner healing. With this gift, there's no need for teasing and testing to see who might be lurking in the corner of some oppressed soul.

As we gained more wisdom in our healing ministry, we came to see that casting out evil spirits in Jesus' name is only part of deliverance. We began to realize how critical it is to identify the area of weakness or sin that grants the demons access to the victim's personality.

In Drew's case, we knew something of his history. We were quick to call down God's blessing and grace to take hold in different areas as we cast out spirits. We arranged follow-up sessions for inner healing and counsel, addressing the specific areas of pain and weakness under the Lord's guidance.

We now realize it would have been better to have started with inner healing and counsel to strengthen the personality and character of Drew. We also recognize now the effectiveness of tonics or spiritual aids in preparing a person for deliverance. For instance, as a Catholic, it would have been helpful for Drew to receive the Eucharist daily as a source of spiritual strength before prayer for deliverance. For all Christians, more personal prayer and more reading of Scripture are effective tonics.

As we look back, we see that we would have called upon the ministry of a priest in praying over Drew. The charism of Holy Orders with its authority would have proved very helpful in praying over this young Catholic who had just returned to the faith.

We thank the Lord that he covered for our inexperience in that early battle for Drew's mind and will. We realized afterwards that we needed to learn care and caution in this area of the healing ministry. The dignity of the human person needs to be safeguarded. The afflicted one shouldn't be needlessly subjected to the abuses of overly zealous amateurs, no matter how noble or compassionate their motivation.

Deliverance is not the sort of thing you should explore out of curiosity, or even out of compassion or zeal. The well-being of others is at stake. Too much spiritual, psychological, and physical damage can be done and—sad to say—has been done by well-meaning efforts to cast out something that wasn't even there in the first place.

We have seen harmful effects when someone takes on this special aspect of the healing ministry without a clear call or an anointing of the Holy Spirit. This sensitive area of the healing ministry really does require unusual sensitivity and special spiritual gifts. Even though all believers have been given the *general* authority to heal and to rebuke demons, common sense and godly wisdom tell us that just as not every Christian will be given the *ministry* of preaching or of community administration, so it is with inner healing, counsel, and deliverance. Everyone does not receive the call to this ministry.

There is, however, a place for deliverance in our lives. When unwanted patterns of thinking, feeling, or behaving don't seem to yield to our best efforts—when healing prayer and godly counsel and sincere contrition find themselves thwarted by obsession in our thought life or compulsion in our behavior: these are signs that deliverance may be needed from the active interference of personal evil in the form of evil spirits.

At this point, a mature and stable Christian ministry team should be consulted. More personal prayer, Scripture reading, fasting, and other spiritual aids or tonics should be considered to prepare the person for deliverance.

We have touched on deliverance very briefly as a subset of the healing ministry. We don't want to draw undue attention to it. And we certainly don't want to treat it as an independent ministry—independent of prayer for healing and counsel.

Let us keep our eyes on Jesus and not on our adversary. Teresa of Avila, one of the great Christian mystics, chided those who were overly concerned about the spiritual battle that she had to wage against Satan in her own life. Her wise response applies as much to us as it did to her worried contemporaries: "Why say, 'Satan, Satan!' when you should be saying, 'Jesus, Jesus!'"

Do you see the need to cry out, "Jesus, Jesus!?" Do you see the need for inner healing in your own life and wonder what you should do next? Or maybe you're wondering whether you really need inner healing? Or maybe you're wondering if you should seek professional help to receive the wholeness and holiness God wants for your life?

We'd like to share some guidelines that can help you discern how inner healing might fit into your life.

TEN

Inner Healing and You

D O YOU WANT TO BE FREED from some hurtful memory
that's been haunting you for years? Do you have an
inability to forgive others because you are harboring
unresolved bitterness and resentment in your heart? Have
you been suffering from a deep emotional wound of the
heart for many years? Do you seem unable to love God
and others because of some emotional or psychological
burden you're carrying? Or maybe someone you love is
weighed down by a problem of this sort, and you'd like to
get him the help he so desperately needs?

Well, be encouraged! God is our loving heavenly
Father. He wants to make you whole and draw you to
himself. You are a child of God, and he desires the very
best for you in his Son Jesus.

Here are some guidelines to consider as you seek him
and his saving grace through inner healing.

1. *You Must Seek God First.* You need to focus on God and
seek his guidance for your life. This is always the first step
in pursuing wholeness and holiness, which is the object of
inner healing. If we settle for anything less, we will miss
the mark and experience dissatisfaction and frustration.

2. *Don't Put the Gift before the Giver.* Like Rick who initially sought deliverance from drug abuse but not salvation in Christ, you will experience frustration if you put the gift of healing before the Lord who is the healer. You may be healed and released from your affliction, but you will only find lasting peace and contentment by putting God first.

3. *Seek God through Daily Prayer and Scripture Reading.* To really seek God and understand his plan for your life, you need to pray daily and read the Word of God. Then he can begin to reveal himself to you. Remember the account of Steve and Nora's marital difficulties? The situation began to improve as Nora turned to the Lord in daily prayer. He began to transform her life and that had an impact on her marriage and on her family life.

4. *As God Leads You in Prayer for Healing, Turn to a Mature Christian.* God doesn't want us to solve our problems on our own. We all need the support of our brothers and sisters in Christ. Seek the advice of a mature Christian you can trust as the Lord gives you wisdom about the need for healing in your life. It is a mistake to diagnose our own problems. We all have our blind spots. In fact, a common tendency in all of us is to exaggerate or overlook our own personal problems.

5. *After Some Guidance, Take a Period of Time to Pray.* Your mature Christian friend has given you some advice or guidance about an area in your life that you think needs inner healing. Take some time to pray about it before the Lord. Take the amount of time that seems right for you. It may be days or weeks, or maybe even a month or more. Let the Lord lead.

6. *Make a Decision.* Decide in the Lord about the area in question. You may want to set a deadline for making a decision. You may decide after some initial guidance and prayer that you really do need inner healing to become the whole and holy person God wants you to be. Now you need to decide to *do* something about it.

7. *Seek Professional Help if You Think You Need It.* You probably need professional help if you are suffering from a foundational insecurity that is rooted in your early years as a child. There's also a strong likelihood you need professional help if your problem has caused you prolonged distress—perhaps in the form of anxiety, depression, or fear. Remember the prolonged distress of Anna, the musician who suffered from bulimia. She was so distraught that she had to take a leave of absence from the conservatory where she was studying. Anna needed professional help.

8. *Seek Counseling and Prayer from a Christian Therapist.* If you need professional help, seek out a Christian therapist who focuses on true wholeness and holiness in his ministry. Don't settle for less. Seek God in prayer and consult mature Christians in the area of counseling and healing as you select a therapist. Spend some time. Do some investigating. There is much confusion in the area of inner healing. It has been contaminated in some quarters by secular influences and by the occult.

9. *How to Pursue Inner Healing without Professional Help.* If you don't think you need professional help but need some prayer for healing, talk to your Christian friends and those in your prayer group, your community, or local church. Talk to them about the area in need of healing.

Ask for prayer. Maybe your prayer group or your church has a prayer team. Contact them and explain the nature of your problem.

10. *Don't Expect Healing to Happen Overnight.* Patiently wait upon the Lord for the healing you think you need. Don't rush it. If you do, you may miss out on marvelous opportunities for growth as you respond to the Lord in your suffering and pain. Remember Ellen's long seven-month wait for healing from parental rejection. A quicker healing would have robbed her of the all-important lesson that God the Father wanted to be ever present to her in every situation of her life.

11. *Appropriate Your Healing by Loving God and Others.* When God heals us, we are able to reach out and love him and each other with a depth and a freedom that we would never have thought possible. This is an important way of fully appropriating the healing God has for us. Recall the poignant example we drew from our own family. Our son, John, decided to risk his own life for our only daughter Claire when they were both caught in that sudden squall off the coast of Maine where we were vacationing. It proved to be a moving example of how God was healing all of us as a family through our agape love for each other.

12. *Have Expectant Faith that God Will Act in Your Life.* We also shared with you how important expectant faith proved in helping our family appropriate the healing God wanted for us. Don't let negative attitudes or lies from the evil one rob you of God's will and plan for your life. Stand

in expectant faith and expect to see God act. If necessary, ask others in your prayer group or church to pray over you for a greater measure of faith.

13. *Be Open to God's Healing Action in Your Life.* Even if you don't see an immediate need for inner healing in your life, be open to God's healing touch. No one is perfectly whole or holy in this earthly life. We can all use more of God's saving and healing grace in our lives. Remember Matt who lost his only grandson and experienced a profound sense of loss. He had lived a happy and a fruitful life for sixty-four years. Matt didn't experience his need for healing and wholeness until he lost his grandson. Yet after his healing, Matt experienced a dimension of wholeness and holiness he had never even thought he needed!

14. *Develop an Eternal Perspective on Life.* All of us, particularly as we seek healing, need to keep our sights set on heaven. We need to keep firmly in mind that this mortal world is passing away. Complete wholeness and holiness will never be ours until we enter heaven and see the Lord face to face. This means it is far more important to be right with God than to be healed of affliction.

15. *Pursue Holiness of Life.* Ultimately, what really matters is that all of us pursue holiness of life. We need to desire God first and the things of his kingdom. This is the goal of inner healing because holiness of life enables us to live for God. It enables us to become whole, lovable people in the service of Jesus, our master and king. We begin to love God and others as we are loved.

May the grace of inner healing help us all to grasp our identity as sons and daughters of God, so that we can give ourselves completely to God in Christ for his glory. Our prayer is that Christ's all-merciful love, poured out upon a sad and selfish world, will not return to him void but will accomplish the saving purposes of God the Father in all of our lives. This is our prayer for inner healing which, from the beginning to the end, is a grace for holiness.

Other Books of Interest
from Servant Books

Healing Principles
Michael Scanlan, T.O.R.

Out of the wide variety of healing ministries active today,
what really works? Are there any basic rules to follow? What if
you've tried every technique you can think of, but there are
still no results? For fifteen years, Michael Scanlan has been
actively involved in the healing ministry. As a result of these
years of experience and observation, *Healing Principles* gives
a clear summary of the ten dynamic principles of the healing
power of the Holy Spirit. *$1.95*

Knowing You Are Loved
John Guest

Many people pay lip service to the statement "God is love,"
without fully experiencing that love in their own lives. In
Knowing You Are Loved, John Guest brings the truth of God's
intimate love into sharper focus. He points out that none of
us can truly love until we know that we are loved by the most
important person in the world—by God himself. Here is real
help for those who need to know God's love more deeply and
more profoundly. *$5.95*